Backwoods Mates
to Hollywood's Greats

Also by Mike Tomkies

Books
Alone in the Wilderness
Between Earth and Paradise
A Last Wild Place
My Wilderness Wildcats
Liane – A Cat from the Wild
Out of the Wild
Golden Eagle Years
On Wing and Wild Water
Moobli
Last Wild Years
In Spain's Secret Wilderness
Wildcat Haven (new and revised edition)
Wildcats
Rare, Wild and Free

Biography
The Big Man (The John Wayne Story)
It Sure Beats Working (The Robert Mitchum Story)

Unpublished Novels
Let Ape and Tiger Die
Today the Wolf is Dead

Autobiography
My Wicked First Life

Videos and DVDs
Eagle Mountain Year
At Home with the Eagles
Forest Phantoms
My Barn Own Family
River Dancing Year
Wildest Spain
Wildest Spain Revisited
Last Eagle Years
My Bird Table Theatres
My Wild 75th Summer
My Wild 80th Year

Backwoods Mates
to Hollywood's Greats

Mike Tomkies

Whittles Publishing

Published by
Whittles Publishing,
Dunbeath,
Caithness KW6 6EY,
Scotland, UK
www.whittlespublishing.com

© Text and photographs 2009 Mike Tomkies
ISBN 978-1904445-83-8

Printed by
InPrint, Latvia

Contents

1

Into the Unknown

I was now totally alone, 5,000 miles from all I'd known, and the main emotion I felt as I drove up the wild, forested road in an old Pontiac car I'd bought shortly after leaving Vancouver airport was fear. Sheer unadulterated fear. I had abandoned my hedonistic big-city life as a London-based show business writer, not only because I had become disillusioned with that life, and the very noise of the city, but because I wanted to live in a quiet, pure, wild place far away, and write the 'great novel' for which I had been making notes for months. The final trigger for my departure came when the beautiful actress I was hoping to marry signed a contract for a big TV series that stipulated she couldn't marry for three years, although we had agreed to meet again once I'd finished the book. Above all, at 38 years of age I wanted to escape popular journalism and make my final stand to be a writer. Alone, in a strange wild place, I felt I could achieve this. But my first impressions of western Canada made me feel utterly alien and scared, and I even thought briefly of fleeing back to the airport and the easy sheltered life I'd known.

As I drove along, the great mountains returned my first looks of awe with contempt, staring down from beneath their skullcaps of snow like great old gods, the custodians of an ancient primitive treasure. British Columbia has a stark grandeur that at first flays the mind of a city-conditioned man. This vast province, almost as large as central Europe, was in the mid 1960s the last free frontier left in the western world. Untamed forests clothed colossal mountains in areas half the size of England, some still untouched by man. Bounded in the east by the Rockies, and licked and battered in the west by the mighty Pacific, its coastline was an intricate maze of islands and wild rocky inlets, some reaching inland for ninety miles. The sea and rivers abounded with five species of salmon, among which a seventy pounder was no rare catch. British Columbia was also a gargantuan, indifferent land with waterfalls higher than Niagara, log jams that could dam up lakes for six miles, cataclysmic forest fires that could clear fifty miles of high timber in a week, and a land in whose great vastness grizzly bears and cougars – the last of the great North American carnivores – found their only real stronghold. In this great wilderness I had to find a peaceful place in which to write.

My attempts to find a cabin drew a blank on the first day, and as I spent the night dozing across the front seat of the Pontiac in a secluded forest glade I was sure I had made a big mistake. But on the second day, after enquiries at the store in the third little fishing village, and at a bar called 'The Riggers Roost' in the beer parlour, some friendly loggers put me on to what seemed the ideal cabin. It was a sprawling wooden bungalow down a private track, isolated, and tucked away amid cedar, fir and arbutus trees on a small promontory above the sea. The view was idyllic, with three tree-covered islets half a mile from the shore, within easy reach of any rowboat I would buy for fishing. The owner was working up in the Yukon, but after several late-night phone calls he agreed that I could have the cabin for a reasonable rent. The only drawback was that I'd have to vacate it for a month after the first ten days, as he had already let the place to some Americans for their summer holiday.

I spent those first ten days plotting the form of my novel. Not sure where to go on the day I had to vacate, I went back to the beer parlour, where I'd made casual friends after a couple more visits. They told me about a cheap duplex apartment down in Gunsmith Bay that would be empty for a couple of weeks. It would have to do.

Whoever built that duplex was certainly no carpenter. The walls were of the flimsiest plywood, and for most of my first two nights I was kept awake by a beery young couple who spent the darkened hours alternating between violent arguments and the impassioned grunts and squeals of lusty love. Fascinating, but unfortunately it left the unwilling listener more tired than it did the participants.

On the third night, unable yet again to do any writing because of the healthy honeymooning racket next door, I again visited the beer parlour, there to treat my gullet to the acidic sleep-inducer that Canadian parlours call 'draught beer'. Lost in a haze of smoke and beer, dazed by the strange talk of big fish and big trees, and unable to contribute much myself – because none of these men were vaguely interested in Britain or Europe – I listened, the duly enraptured immigrant. Suddenly I was aware of a crushing handshake, and of being introduced to a man called Big Jim. He loomed above the table, large, blue-eyed and ruddy, his shirt sleeves rolled high, his arms oil-stained from wrestling with the engine of his boat, which now lay in the harbour.

"This guy's got nothing to do for a month. He'll go with you," said one of my new pals at the table. Big Jim's eyes ranged over me for a moment, then fixed mine with a friendly stare. "Is that true?"

"What? Is what true?" I replied. I didn't know what was going on, and was suspicious. "Go where?"

The big man laughed. "Look, I just bought a fish collector. I'm heading up the coast to buy salmon. I came here to meet a pal who was to work with me, but he's taken off for Vancouver with a big roll and a dame. He could be away a coupla weeks, and I don't have time to hang around. Okay?"

"I'm interested," I said.

"Let's go talk."

We moved to a small, quiet table, and Big Jim – Jim Olson, a third-generation Canadian of Norwegian blood – put me in the picture. For the past three years he'd worked as a mate and then finally a skipper on the big fish packer boats that plied the waters up and down that wild coast, loading up with fish from the shore stations and running them to the canning factories in Vancouver, and on Vancouver Island. His days as a skipper had ended the day *his* mate had fallen asleep on watch, and the boat had run aground. Big Jim had shouldered the blame, but after the mud had stopped flying he had resigned, determined to go into business on his own.

He had then acquired one of Vancouver's oldest and smallest ferry boats, which he'd hoped to turn into a floating night club. But after running foul of British Columbia's puritanical drink and licensing laws, the venture had failed. Next, Jim had invented a clam digger, which had picked up scores of pleasingly round pebbles but very few clams. Now, with what was left of his capital, plus the help of an optimistic bank manager, Jim had bought the *Seamoat*, a small, tug-like craft that could carry six tons of fish in its hold. His plan seemed simple: with virtually no overheads, and no home to keep up (he was unmarried, and could live on the boat), he could tootle into the dozens of tiny fish ports up the wild coast, buy up surplus fish from the little trollers and gill-netters – most of whose owners he knew – and run the fish to the shore packers. But he needed a helper: to load fish, to set them in the ice, and to help run the boat.

"Can't pay you much," said Jim. "Still paying off for the boat. Are you on?"

I thought of the duplex in Gunsmith Bay. I thought of the high mountain that towered above it, and how, when the sun went behind it at four in the afternoon, the whole bay went dark and gloomy. I thought of the couple next door, and the plywood walls. I wasn't getting much writing done there. Besides, I was tired of writing, and here was a unique chance to learn about what seemed an extraordinary way of life.

"I'm on," I said.

"Right, we'll go grab your sleeping bag and stuff. We'll leave in the morning."

2

With the Lusty Men of the Salmon

The *Seamoat* was fat, black and ugly, and as she leaned her obese thirty-foot bulk against the wooden wharf it seemed as if she never wanted to leave it again.

Considering the night had been spent in a bag on top of a pile of canvas on a hard bench in the black foc'sle, I had slept quite well. At 5.30 am I woke to the clanging of knife on frying pan, and Jim's grinning face from the hatch informing me that he had fixed breakfast. Crawling gingerly and guiltily out – I had intended to take care of all the cooking on the trip – I dashed cold water over the beginnings of a beard, tried to look as if I didn't feel bad, and took the heavily laden tin plate Jim was holding out.

"We don't get much sleep on these trips," he said gruffly. "Figure we can get enough of that when we're ashore with the girls."

I said okay, appreciating his rough tact, and then stared in disbelief at the plate. Jim's idea of breakfast was unique. It consisted of layers of hot, fried pancakes. On the first layer was a slice of ham. The second was covered with strawberry jam. On this lay a third hot pancake covered with maple syrup, and in the syrup sat a fried egg.

"It's a Billy Mandrake sandwich," said Jim. "Named after the guy who invented it. Tomato ketchup is optional." As I watched, he picked up a bottle and poured ketchup all over the horrendous mixture.

"Of course!" I said, following suit. At least it must be pulsating with vitamins, and one look at the deep black hold, the ancient fish scales and the huge one-prong pitchforks we would be using to load the big salmon aboard told me I would need all the vitamins I could get. Somehow I gulped it all down.

Jim push-buttoned the 150 Palmer diesel into life. I cast off the rope hawsers, and went back to wash up and sweep out the wheelhouse. As the *Seamoat* slid gently out of the harbour on the start of our 400-mile journey, I still could hardly believe I'd signed on as a deckhand on this battered old tub. I joined Jim at the wheel, where he obviously was feeling good to be in command of his own boat. The moon was still out in the early dawn, and as we headed up the Strait of Georgia the coal-black water danced, white-flecked, and the moonlight turned the trees to feathery grey upon innumerable passing islands. Flashes of jade, orange and purple rock shone into our window, and around us fish were leaping like brilliant ghosts.

"Looks like a good run of Coho heading for the inlets," Jim said, sucking happily at his pipe.

He gave me the wheel, told me to keep to centre channel, and talked about the life led by the wild, dour men of the salmon. At that time the fishermen of British Columbia provided nearly half of Canada's total fisheries wealth, and of all the fish, the salmon was king. "Though the halibut men up north might give you an argument on that!" Jim smiled.

In these waters there are five basic breeds of salmon: the Spring (also known as Tyee, King, Chinook and Blackmouth), the Coho (also known as Silver and Blueback), the Pink, the Sockeye and the Chum. To pluck these fish from the crystal seas for the dinner plates of the world, the fishermen had three main methods – trolling, gill-netting and seine-netting. Trolling was then the most popular, as the thirty-foot gulf trolling boats could be run by one man, and there were many lone wolves in this free, non-unionised industry (as it then was). These boats had two trolling arms: from motor winches on deck the lines went out through three pulleys on each arm, and were held vertical in the water by forty-pound weights shaped like cannon balls. To each line were clipped three or four nylon leaders that had chromium 'flashers' to attract the fish, and the line ended with hooks on which were threaded brightly coloured plastic lures called 'hootchy kootchies'. Another line went out from the main mast. In total, a good troller could tow as many as thirty lures through the sea at once.

"When the fish bite," said Jim, "the bells on the trolling arms ring and you winch the fish in. If you hit into a good run the boat suddenly sounds like a great goddam alarm clock!" It didn't sound like the dainty fly fishing I had known in Britain.

The gill-netters were wider-beamed boats that could be run by up to four men, and they worked mainly in the shallower narrows. The net, from a power drum in the stern, was dropped over with an anchor and a flagged buoy, and then paid out across the water, held up by floats. The boat waited at one end until a run of salmon hit the net and got their gills stuck in the mesh. Then the whole net was winched in on the drum, and the men pulled the fish out by hand. It was tough on the fingers.

The seine-netters made the biggest hauls. They were larger boats, which cruised about in the straits or the open sea until they ran into a school of salmon. Swiftly, the big purse net was run around the school on floats, and when it was full the lines were tightened, closing the net like a purse. Then the whole thing was winched aboard by a power boom. At the end of a good season these seiner crews could divide profits of $30,000 between them – big money in the mid 1960s. These fishermen could often afford winters in Hawaii.

After four hours of steady chugging we were in Fairview, the port for the mill town of Powell River. There we were due to meet the *Lady Luck*, a sea packer that was to fill our holds with ice. As we tied up, a big, swarthy, thickset man two boats away hailed Jim by name.

"It's Jack Silva," said Jim, as we walked over. "Half Portuguese, half Indian. A madman, but one of the best gill-netters alive. He once axed down a packer station door to get his fish into ice at three in the morning!"

Jack was moodily mending a hole in his net. His fingers were like black bananas from hauling the fish from its mesh. Each finger was about an inch thick: I had never seen such hands. "Hey, you old dog," he said to Jim, "haven't seen you round here since you beached the *Ballena*!"

"You heard about that, eh?" said Jim sitting down. "Yeah, that Ed fell asleep on me; shoved us up a sandbank."

"Ed Foley? You kidding! He did that to me too. I told the guy to wake me the minute he felt tired, but he said he was okay. Half an hour later we hit hard in Granite Bay. Low tide, luckily – another ten foot either way and we'd have lost the boat. I kicked his ass off at Alert Bay. Hear he's down town now."

"Yeah," said Jim. "He's with the brokers. Funny how the guy always lands on his feet. What you doing so far down, Jack?"

Jack dropped his net, spat silently into the water. "The wife's mother's ill. I've been here three days. Wish to hell she'd either kick the bucket or get well." He got up and washed his hands in a bucket of seawater. "Got nothing against the old girl," he added apologetically. "But she's gone ninety, and we're missing some good runs up at Blackfish. You goin' up there?"

"Yep," said Jim. "Waiting for ice from the *Lady L.*"

"Won't be in 'til tonight. Just heard over the air."

"Hell!" said Jim, "I wanted to be out of here this afternoon."

We weren't out of there that afternoon. It was five o'clock before the *Lady Luck* loomed up and its skipper hailed Jim from the bridge. We tied the *Seamoat* alongside, and within minutes the big boat's power boom was scooping up netfuls of ice and dumping them into our hold. I tried to keep pace with it and shovel it all into the shelves where our salmon were to be laid. In two hours we had all the ice we needed. I looked up, perspiring. "Got enough?" asked the baby-faced young giant called Dick who had been directing the ice net out of *Lady L*'s hold.

"Yeah, that'll do 'er," I said, trying to sound like I'd been at such work all my life.

He stood up, shoved the net away, and sang "Oh, bend down and touch your toes. I'll show you where the wild goose goes!" Someone laughed, there was a sudden whoosh of water, and he staggered back, drenched. "What … who the hell? …" He stared all round him – up into the empty crow's nest, behind the bridge. Nothing. Everyone was quietly doing what they had to do. No-one had seen a thing. As Dick staggered below, mouthing curses, to get some dry clothes, Jim clapped me on the back and said the drinks were on him.

The beer parlour was a vast wooden hangar painted a curdled cream, and was full of mill workers and fishermen. They were drinking the way they used to in the Australian outback bars when closing time was 6 pm.

The floors were awash with beer and sawdust, and there was only one woman in the place. She was old but tough, almost as wide as she was tall, and large jowls made her face seem almost two feet long. She wore a short-sleeved blue blouse and black lace gloves that came halfway up her arms. As I watched, she shrieked with laughter and whacked the nearest man on the back, knocking him clean off his chair. As he climbed back, laughing, I felt I had stepped into an old-time western movie. Everyone, as BC law required, was sitting down round wooden tables, not allowed to stand up and drink, and every table seemed its own bedlam. "Ya want *two*?" asked the waiter. "Yeah, make it two," said Bud, the skipper of the *Lady Luck*. The waiter stuck two beers before each of us, and everyone got their money out and put it on the table, as was drinking custom. The waiter didn't choose mine.

"Listen," I said, still puzzled. "What happened to your man back there?"

They all roared with laughter, and Bud said "That Dick. That so-called student: he gives me too much stick, so tonight he got it." They all laughed again. Bud sank the last of his first glass, banged it on the table, and picked up his second.. "Goddammit, I should have been up here this morning. In Vancouver they think the fish business runs itself at weekends. Those cocksucking religious… they pay their bit to the church and think they're all good men." Then he added with contempt: "Playin' golf on Saturdays!"

Jack Silva commiserated, and told us of the time he'd had to axe that packer station door down, to get his fish into ice one Sunday dawn. "They got a guy there every Sunday *now*!" he added with satisfaction.

"Heard about that," said Bud. "You did the right thing, Jack, but they know downtown it was you."

"Figured they did."

"Ah, they'll not bother a top high liner like Jack," said Jim, dodging Jack's embarrassed playful swipe. "They *need* guys who book in 25,000 bucks of fish a year."

Jack sighed, and spat into the sawdust. "Too many shore packers are run by retired business guys who buy a marina and reckon they can shut up shop at the end of office hours. For Chrissakes, we work twenty-four hours round the clock, and when we arrive with fish there's no-one up."

"Yeah," agreed Bud. "And the other thing is there's too many young guys – greenhorns. They don't understand the business and don't want to. They're in it for a few bucks, then off back to college. They try to save on wages by using these guys, but in these seas they're often a danger to your life."

"Can't the unions stop that?" I asked in all innocence.

"Unions!" laughed Bud. "What unions? These guys ain't gonna join no union. That's why they're fishermen! They're all individualists, each guy his own boss. You can't organise 'em. That's the whole goddamn joy of it."

Just then the young giant called Dick came in and joined us – in dry clothes. No-one mentioned his ducking. Another double round of drinks came up, but still the waiter ignored my proffered money, and this time took Jim's. "There's more than fifty million people in his little country," said Jim, referring to Britain and looking at me. "And *all* the working folk are in unions. Ain't that right, Mike?"

One of the reasons why I'd left Britain was the frequent strikes, including a recent dock strike – and my belongings had still not arrived. I told them what I could about British unions: how many people felt the unions' original *raison d'être* had gone, and how now, by striking for more wages for shorter hours, and by doing so on the slightest pretext, they were in a way exploiting their own hard-up country.

"Sounds a sick place to me," said Jack. Then followed a heated discussion in which young Dick, who was an economics student, made animated contributions.

It was a long, happy, hard-drinking night, the talk being that of men who drank hard but worked a great deal harder. They were proud, simple men, full of stories of beached and holed boats, of the big new canning factory that could clear 250,000 pounds of herring in an hour, of log booms that burst adrift and broke the nets, of killer whale pods, of sports fishermen who'd been drowned in the dreaded Yucataw Rapids (through which we were going to pass), and of the wild characters of the past, some of whom were now forgotten men living on that past in Skid Road, Vancouver.

As everyone was being turned out of the beer parlour, Bud sank the last of his beer, looked over, and said quietly, "Jim, have you any idea how difficult it is to get a bucket of water up to the crow's nest without being seen?"

Dick yelled "It was *you*, you bastard!", whipped off his cap, and whacked Bud a good-natured blow across the chest with it. "For that I'm comin' in tomorrow for more pay!"

"Dick," replied Bud with magnificent aplomb, "I have very few pleasures left in life – very few. For thirty years I've been nothing but a fisherman, plying these waters with fish boats, collectors and packers. I've been up to my eyeballs in blood and slime … but … one of my greatest pleasures today is underpaying you!"

Then out we all walked into the starry dark night, swaying happily, men among men and ready for our bunks, with me complaining I hadn't even bought a drink, and with Dick shaking his head and thinking up some way to get even with his skipper.

That first day set the pattern for the rest of the trip. When we weren't working hard we were drinking in the beer parlours – but we were not playing about. Jim himself was fighting for economic survival, and time after time, by going into those lost and forgotten parlours up and down that etiolated coastline, we would come out of them late at night and start loading up with salmon from one-man trollers, fish we would never have got by staying outside, respectably sober in our bunks. It was strange for me. I was fresh from pecking at a typewriter, effete with big city life, my own recent decadence, and shovelling ice and pitchforking the big fish into our eight-foot-deep hold was therapy indeed.

At dawn each day we headed for tiny fishing villages with names like Shoal Bay, Salmon Arm, Minstrel Island, Refuge Cove, Blackfish Sound and Mermaid Bay. We drifted day after day, night after night, workers in a strange watery paradise, in a beautiful landscape never to be taken for granted. On our first run to Shoal Bay we took our first salmon aboard. Out of the faint mist loomed a small troller owned by Tommy Pullen, a friend Jim had been hoping to meet. He was a wiry, red-headed Scot, and as we tied together out there, far out of the sight of land, Tommy yelled to his wife in the galley to fix some coffee.

"This guy's even crazier than Silva," Jim told me. "He's always up before the magistrates, mostly for being drunk, but he puts on such a tearful display he nearly always gets off. Yet nobody trolls better than Tommy."

We climbed aboard; he looked an inoffensive little fellow to me. "Good to see you again, Jim," he said. "Heard you were on your way." He eyed our boat. "Hmm, not a bad old tub. I got some sockeye aboard; what you paying?"

"Thirty-three cents." (A pound.)

"Yeah?" He took his teeth out suddenly, and swilled them in seawater coming through a deck hose as he made calculations on his fingers. "Okay then. Hell, I been on the radio all morning and there ain't a packer for miles."

A few minutes later Tommy was lopping over 1,000 pounds of sockeye onto our deck. Jim handed me one of the one-prong pitchforks. "Stick 'em in the gills or the tail," he ordered. "If you hit 'em in the body flesh it comes out of your salary!" Jim weighed the fish on his scales while I forked them down into the icy hold. Picking the heavy fish in the gills or tail is hard, tricky work when they're sliding all over the deck, you're not used to it, and are working with men who've done it all their lives, but we managed to stack all Tommy's fish into ice in half an hour. Then, as I cleaned the blood and slime from my face and clothes, and swabbed the deck, Jim leaped down and stacked the fish more neatly along the shelves, covering each with a layer of ice.

Tommy looked at his watch. "Well, I reckon I can get another half load before it's dark. There's still a few goin' through here." He looked at me. "Wanna come aboard?" I hesitated, but Jim said, "Go ahead. You'll never get a better chance, Mike. See you guys in Shoal Bay."

I jumped aboard the little troller, Jim cast off, and he and the *Seamoat* soon faded away into the mist.

That afternoon I watched a master at work. I'd always thought I knew quite a lot about fishing, but nothing in my life had prepared me for the next two hours. Sitting in the stern, Tommy Pullen first rolled and lit a cigarette. As it flipped about in his lips during a non-stop conversation about fishing, he started his engine, and then let the cannon ball weights down to sixteen fathoms by operating the motor winches with his feet.

As the boat idled along, the cobweb of lines began to string out, so we looked like a galleon without sails. It seemed only moments before the salmon began to hit the lures, the bells were ringing, and Tommy was winching them up, gaffing the big fish, then flicking them off the hooks into the hold and clipping up the empty leaders – each before the next fish came up, and all in one fluid movement. He made it seem a completely effortless procedure, like a magic ballet that miraculously produced fish. Only now and again, when an inert flasher told him the fish was a very big one, did he stop the winch momentarily, stun the fish with a blow from the gaff hook and flick it off, and then on he'd go again.

For a brief while he let me try it, but I would have felt as much at home behind the controls of a jet aircraft. There were twenty things to keep in mind at once – not least the steering, so that the cannon balls didn't foul the rocks – but Tommy was a one-man moving factory, grinning toothless all the while, cigarette still in mouth, extracting only what was apparently his rightful due from the glittering waters. Sometimes we passed sports fishermen in luxury cruisers and I saw their mouths drop open in surprise, their lines hanging empty. To them we were catching fish where none existed. Every salmon that flopped with almost monotonous regularity into the hold was worth a minimum of five dollars to Tommy.

"See how you do it?" he said, suiting his actions to the words. "You winch 'em up, grab the line, haul 'em in, put the gaff against the hook... and... flick... the hook's out and down he drops. Made 2,000 bucks last month. That's good. Made no money last year – well, 1,600. I started late, had a lotta bad luck, got married ..."

"Hey, you want bilge water in your coffee?" yelled his wife from the galley.

"C'mon, I was only kidding, Dana!" He grinned, speaking in an undertone. "Good woman, that. Keeps the boat real spruce. Not many women will live on a boat these days." He spat brown juice overboard. "Not enough room for 'em" Then he raised his voice: *"But she loves it, don't you, Dana?"*

Dana came to the galley door, scoop in hand, a pretty, plump and weather-beaten woman who looked as though she laughed a lot. "Now you've got to be kidding," she said. "Soon as we get our stake, we're clearing outta this." She pointed her scoop. "I'm telling ya now, Tommy!"

Tommy grinned toothlessly at her, made a profuse mock apology, shoved his teeth back in, and expertly dodged the swab she hurled at him. Then he returned to the subject of fish. He hooked a twenty-five-pound Spring from the pile and flicked it towards me.

"The Springs are the best. Know how to tell it from a Coho? In the tail. The Coho's tail is clear but the Spring's is silvery and spotted. Otherwise, when they're the same size, it's hard to know. And the Spring has a much stronger smell. Y'know, a Spring can live to a hundred years and weigh up to ninety pounds? Yeah. Biggest I ever got was seventy-two. The Springs are the only ones who can make it back down the rivers and return to spawn the next year. The Coho, Sockeye and Chum all die after spawning."

After a couple of hours the light started to fade. "Well, that's another 130 bucks," he said. "Not a bad day." Tommy hauled up his lines and we set off for Shoal Bay. As we chugged round Redonda Island, a sports fisherman yelled out, "Hey, Mac, will ya sell me a salmon?" Tommy ignored him. When we were out of earshot he said, "Don't like those damn guys. I fish up in Toba Inlet, and the place is so thick with their boats, sometimes you can't get in. Only one thing to do – run over their lines and put 'em out of business. A man making his living should have right of way."

As we steamed into Shoal Bay Jim was there, busily loading salmon from another troller at the little quay. I jumped aboard to help. The troller, owned by a grizzled old veteran called Jack Bone, seemed to be on its beam ends. His 'sun roof' was a tattered bit of plywood, and strips of torn canvas hung from his booms. His fishing lines were full of knots, yet he seldom got them tangled. He slept on an old mattress, without blankets, with just an old Army coat to cover him. With a wad of fifty-three dollars he'd got from Jim for his fish, Jack stumped off up to the beer parlour.

"You won't believe it," Jim told me, "but that guy's a millionaire. He owns two apartment blocks in Vancouver!"

"We all know it," said Tommy. "But we never let on to Jack we know it! Fifteen years back he just bought that boat and came up here. Hates town. Now me, I can't wait to get back there!"

"Yer darn tootin'," said Dana with feeling. "We're not spending this winter oyster-picking if I have anything to do with it."

"And she has," said Tommy, dodging her slap. "She has!"

I don't recall much of that festive evening. There was a guitar and an accordion, and we drank and danced, and at one stage I sang a Neapolitan song. The proprietor extracted a large fish hook from an old man's thumb, using a tumbler of rye for anaesthetic, whereupon the old man tied a handkerchief round the bleeding digit and joined in the dancing. Tommy bust a table doing a Zorba dance, Jim beat everyone at shuffle-board, and I was informed from the depths of foaming tankards that any time I got a boat, I was assured of a berth at Shoal Bay. I think the only thing that stopped me becoming a free-boating fisherman right then was that one had to be a Canadian citizen to get a commercial licence, and that could take up to five years.

Before we turned in, Jim checked his cashbox. To my surprise it contained over $3,000 in notes.

"Most of these guys prefer cash," Jim explained. "But I always get them to *book* their fish if I can. In the long run it's better for them. A guy gets much better credit if the company can see he's booked in some 12,000 bucks of fish in a year."

My surprise increased when I saw a revolver beside the notes. Jim took out the gun, checked it, and put it back. "Where we're going," he said cryptically, "we may need it!" He didn't explain further.

At five next morning we headed north-east for Bute Inlet. Despite the shenanigans of the previous night, Jim had gleaned the vital fact that there were heavy Sockeye runs up there. Only old Jack was awake as Jim looked at the sleeping boats around us and said, "These guys should be out there in the Straits right now. They should wander more and anchor at night, not hang around here."

Jack agreed. He was off on a three-day trip himself. He was one of the last real lone-wolf fishermen, the ones who made the most. His tattered boat was equipped with brine freezer tanks, and he just wandered, letting down his hook at nights and sleeping wherever he happened to be. "Don't worry Jim," he grinned. "We'll have fish for you when you head back through."

We chugged along at near full speed for some two hours, and as we neared Deep Water Bay Jim said he hoped there would be one or two Japanese 'high liner' fishermen there with full loads aboard. "Stray Japs" was the phrase he used. To me his words were reminiscent of the Pacific campaign in World War II. But sure enough, as we came into the bay proper, one of the top Japanese boats lay at anchor. Beautifully kept, with its brass rails gleaming in the sun, it sat low in the water. Jim judged it to be full of fish.

It was now that I saw Jim adopt his 'psychological approach' to get the Jap's fish from him. Bringing the *Seamoat* close in to the Jap he noisily bought a small load of Sockeye from another small troller, deliberately ignoring Billy Sakata, the Jap, who came out onto his bridge to watch us. Suddenly, after a long pause, he called across: "Hey, what are you paying for Red Spring?"

Jim winked at me and turned round. "Is it troll or net?" (An undamaged Red Spring caught on the troll was worth ten cents a pound more than one damaged by netting.)

"Troll," said Sakata.

"Okay, sixty cents." Jim knew the fish *must* have been netted, because the Jap was a gill-netter, but he could always retract his offer if the fish had been damaged too heavily.

"I got a thirty pounder," said Sakata, and he heaved the fish up. It was in good condition. Jim paid him his eighteen dollars in cash, flourishing the notes. This meant Sakata had made three dollars fifty more than he would have made from his own packer for that one fish, but Jim showed it on his books as having paid fifty cents a pound for a netted Red Spring. The extra came from his own pocket. But it was clever business, for by now he had the Jap hooked. Sakata had a further 2,000 pounds of Sockeye aboard, and he was greedy now he had found a good buyer. He sold us 1,550 pounds of Sockeye at forty-three cents a pound (six cents more than he would have got from his own company) and still kept 150 fish back to keep his own packer happy. So, by giving the Jap three dollars over the top for the one Red Spring, Jim had also secured the load of Sockeye, which, with his collector's profit of six cents a pound, meant he'd made over ninety dollars inside an hour.

"You've got to know the psychology of the Japs," said Jim as we chugged away. "They're completely different from the Canadian boys. You can't *tell* them anything, only plant the seed."

By now the *Seamoat* was almost full, and we decided to unload the salmon at a packer station at Campbell River, but before that we spent a luxurious evening in the town's best hotel and got cleaned up. Jim took the chance to ring his fiancée, who worked as a secretary in Vancouver. He came back from the phone with a long face. "She's getting a holiday in a couple of weeks; wants to come on the boat. Says I promised her. Hell, I must have been stoned."

"Well, if she's marrying you," I said, "she ought at least know what your life is like."

"Yeah," agreed Jim, without too much enthusiasm.

Next day we headed up towards Blackfish Sound, taking a few fish aboard at two tiny coves, and it was around one in the morning when we reached the rapids near Stuart Island, where boats had been smashed and men had drowned in the treacherous whirlpools. Here, if you went in on a wrong fast tide, your boat could be whirled round a couple of times and sucked down some ten feet before, if you were lucky, the whirlpool released you. Even experienced tugboat skippers had lost sections of log booms here.

It was moonlight again as we came up to the rapids. Jim handed me the wheel, and went to the bows to take a closer look at the incoming tide with which we were running. "She's okay," he said as he came back; then, to my astonishment, he threw himself down on his bunk with his favourite sandwich of jam and peanut butter and shouted, "Keep to the centre, and take us through!"

Jim had a strange sense of humour at times. I reasoned he'd hardly hand the wheel to me if there was any real danger, but then again, watching him on his bunk with a bottle of beer in one hand and that idiotic sandwich in the other, I was none too sure. Somehow I got us through, with a pounding heart, and with the boat waltzing from side to side as if at a drunken barn dance.

3

Flipping for Whacks

The further north we went, and the further from civilisation, the wilder the life of the men in the half-forgotten outposts became. They had their own moral code, and a rough, fundamental justice that bore little relation to the highly systematised morality I'd known in the big cities of Europe or America. A man who tampered with another man's wife was liable to find bullets kicking up the dust around his cabin next morning. Such matters would be settled arbitrarily by the local Mounties, men usually renowned for their sense of fair play – not to mention their ability to hand out a belting right to the jaw. Courts were seldom used, because in most places there weren't any. There was such a babble of tongues in these northern beer parlours that it was hard to understand what many of the men were trying to say: among the basic Scots and Irish loggers, fishermen and miners there were 'New Canadians' who'd come from Germany, Finland, Sweden, Portugal, Italy, Poland, Greece and even Syria. Most everyone belonged to a minority and each group had its favourite jokes about the others, with the Poles and the local Indians bearing the brunt of these.

One night we were in a beer parlour that overlooked some narrow-neck rapids, when I heard shouts from outside. A group of Indians were heading down the rapids in a big canoe that seemed crazily out of control. I was sure they were yelling for help, and pointed them out to Jim. He looked out of the window, and grinned.

"Oh, it's just those drunken Church House Indians," he said blandly. "They're always in trouble. They'll just hit a rock and spill out. They're okay."

No-one up there apparently bothered about a bunch of drunken Indians. As a group, the coastal Indians were known for their inability to hold their liquor. But also, while there were a few pockets of Indians who hadn't adjusted to the changes that commercial fishing, logging and mining had brought to what was once their land, there were many who *did* excel at these pursuits. The best high riggers – men who climbed with lifebelt and spurs to top the big trees – were often Haida Indians.

The one thing all these men had in common was that they lived and worked in the largest unexploited land frontier left in the western hemisphere, and what they did was vital to its future as well as to their own. It bound them together in a rough camaraderie. Most came from tired lands elsewhere, and now, forced to change their own national concepts, were not only developing this wild, virgin land but were creating from its abundant seas, its enormous forests and its almost untouched mineral resources a new national life of their own. They were a rough and ready bunch, but they were also the last of the true pioneers.

The biggest offence was when a man stole an unfair advantage over his fellows. That night the fishermen were talking about a persistent poacher who had just been jailed for two years. He'd been going out at night with just a hand line, and no-one could understand how he would come back next day with a boatload of salmon. One night a fisheries officer went out after dark and slid, lightless, to where he could watch. The old poacher was paying Indians to short-net the Coho in the shallow rapids, a practice legal only for certain Indians, and that only for their own tables. All agreed: the old cheat had got what he deserved.

Several days later, as we headed along the top east coast of Vancouver Island, we accidentally met up with Tommy Pullen again, and he had a full load of Coho aboard. "Can't let you have 'em all Jim," he said, "my regular packer's coming through. Got to keep the book open. But I could let you have half."

Jim agreed; he wanted to keep some room in our hold anyway, for fish we would buy on the way back.

"Okay," said Tommy, "where you headed now?"

"Inert Bay," said Jim.

Tommy did a double-take, his face registering shock. "Inert Bay!" he gasped. "Are you kidding?"

"No," said Jim, his back to me. "No trip up this coast is complete without visiting Inert Bay."

Tommy looked at him, then away to me, then back to Jim. A slow grin of understanding spread across his face. "Yeah," he said, "that's right. We'll come along with you." The grin became a guffaw, and he slapped his thigh. "Yeah!"

Jim refused to enlarge on this enigmatic conversation as we headed on, with Tommy close behind. The events of the past ten days should perhaps have conditioned me for Inert Bay, but they hadn't. As we steamed into the harbour, Jim chose a deserted spot on the wooden wharf at which to tie up. The few fishermen who were still on their boats in the gathering dusk didn't greet us like they had in other ports of call. As we helped Tommy tie alongside to unload his fish, I noticed that most of the wooden buildings on the hill up from the quay had a battered look, as if they'd been victims of heavy storms. From the biggest of them came an effusion of light and noise, like a wild hillbilly party, powered by drums and concertinas.

"That," said Jim with unusual emphasis, "is the beer parlour."

"And *some* beer parlour!" said Tommy, who was already slapping his fish onto our decks with what seemed unseemly haste. Once I had forked some four hundred pounds of Coho into our hold, Jim roped the hatch down over them without bothering to lay them flat on the ice shelves. He'd never done that before.

"You'll be booking this lot, eh, Tommy?" he asked, taking down his credit ledger.

"You bet your goddamned life I'm booking 'em!" said Tommy with heat, as he too roped down his hatch. "Tonight I'm only taking beer money with me!"

Just then Dana emerged from their cabin with a determined but worried look, and handed Tommy a key. "Lock me in," she said. "And if you get into trouble again, don't bother to come home." Tommy grinned at her, and assured her he'd stay out of trouble. Then, with an action that seemed to belie his words, he suddenly pulled out his teeth, handed them to her, and winced theatrically as she slammed the door on him. He locked it as she had instructed. We walked to the parlour.

"Take it easy tonight, eh, Tommy?" said Jim.

"Yeah," said Tommy with a quick, vanishing smile. They both had that look on their faces that fighters get when leaving the dressing room for the ring.

As Jim pushed the door open, the full blast of the noisy saloon hit us. Most of the men were built like grizzlies. They looked like they had jackets on when they were only wearing shirts. At a nearby table one of four men spun a nickel. It hit the table, then bounced to the floor. All four studied it. "Jesus!" said the man opposite. Then they all sat bolt upright. The man who'd lost the spin put his hands on the table and turned his head slightly sideways, presenting his jaw. The other drew back his right first, lashed out and struck him, knocking him back slightly. "Hell!" said the stricken man, shaking his head. "You can still hit!" Then he picked up the coin and spun it and it came down heads on the table. "Screw!" said the man who'd struck the blow. Again all the men sat bolt upright. This time the man who'd been hit first struck his opponent, almost knocking him off his chair.

"Saturday night at Inert Bay," said Tommy, shaking his head with a grin and paying for the double round.

"What is it, some kind of game?" I asked, dazed.

"Yeah," said Jim. "It's called Flipping for Whacks. They play it here and at Minstrel Island. But you've got to hit staying upright. And you can't dodge. The trick is to ride the blow. Want to play?"

"No, I don't!" I said hastily. To me, unless I was absolutely forced into a corner, violence was to be avoided at all costs. I couldn't see it as a *game*. Yet here, in this outlandish spot, violence had become fun – a gutsy, lusty way of life by which men, deprived of women's company in the log and fish camps, could let off steam.

In the corner nearest us two Indians started to wrestle drunkenly on the floor. When they kicked a table, scattering drinks, a huge waiter, himself as big as anyone in the bar, yelled at them and broke the fight up.

"Lousy fighters, Indians," said Tommy with contempt. "Always startin' what they can't finish." As he said it, I saw one of the Indians look daggers at him.

We ordered some meat pies. The waiter brought them – without knives or forks. "They don't allow cutlery in here," said Jim. "Someone always starts hurling it around. See over there..." I followed his nod towards the 'Ladies and Escorts' section, in which three middle-aged couples were drinking. Near to them sat two plump Indian squaws, one of whom smiled, black-toothed, at me. "Last time they served knives in here one guy leaped over that partition and knifed a guy with one of those squaws. Never served cutlery since!"

Noticing that the bar had a huge sag in its middle, I went to buy some cigarettes and tested it with my hand. It sank slightly, and was made of plastic. "That's right," Jim confirmed, "plastic and plywood. That's because it gets bust every Saturday night. They got a whole barn full of plastic bars out back. They put in a new one every Monday. This is the night the loggers come out of the trees and beat up the fishermen."

"*Try* to beat up the fishermen," said Tommy, who was getting a mad, predatory look in his eye.

We drank some more, and the animal noise of the place seemed to increase, as if it had a life of its own. It swelled from the loud stomping music, and from throats inflamed by alcohol, until one by one the eyes of the men around us lit up with the same mad look as in Tommy's.

Suddenly one of the squaws flat-footed in from the women's section and slapped a man on the nearby table. "You son of a bitch," she said. "You gave me a couple of baking powder coupons in the dark last week!" The waiter rushed over, and as he told her to get back to her own section, she glared at him. "What's the matter with you, Jack? You screwed me lotsa times too!"

As the waiter shepherded her back, one of the Indians got up and said something to the waiter, who promptly shoved him back into his chair. Two more Indians leaped up and grabbed the waiter, one kicking him in the groin. It was the signal the whole place had been waiting for. Whooping with joy, men banged down their drinks and leaped over tables to join in the fray. A couple of fishermen heaved one of the tables into the fighting mass, pushing it into a corner. Behind us the table full of Indians stood up en masse, and as they ran towards the battle, the one who had looked at Tommy earlier cuffed the back of his head and stood back, waiting.

"Goddam!" said Tommy, glaring down at the table.

"Take it easy, pal," said Jim.

"Come on, white bum. I show you who lousy fighter," said the Indian, weaving about and flailing his arms. Just as Tommy was getting up to fight, Jim shot to his feet, grabbed the Indian from behind and threw him across a table. The man fell onto his back, rolled over, took one look at Jim's angry bulk, and then ran off to join his friends in the fracas by the bar. By now Tommy was really wound up, and took off after the Indian, but as he got near the struggling group a vast French Canadian stepped out of the melee, held up a hand the size of a dinner plate, and shouted, "Not you! You're not one of us. Get back and watch. This is only among friends!"

Tommy stopped, stupefied. Before he could think what to do next, Jim caught hold of him from behind and towed him back towards the door, trying to calm him down. "I tell you Tommy," he said, "you get stuck into that lot and Dana'll leave you for sure."

This seemed to sober Tommy up a little, because by the time Jim had got him abreast of our table the mad look had started to fade from his eyes. "Ay, you're right," he said finally. "Damn bloody Indians, just ain't worth it!"

At the door Jim paused, and we all looked back. The fighting group seemed all arms and legs, with now and again a chair being hurled into the centre from outside. Sometimes a man spun away, bloody nosed, stood momentarily as if he'd been thrown from a warm house into blinding hail, and then leaped back in again, trying to climb back into the middle over the backs of the outer ring of punching men. Suddenly the whole group surged backwards and fell into the bar, which disintegrated gracefully beneath them.

"Ah," said Jim, with evident satisfaction, "*that* was what I wanted you to see. Never would've forgiven myself if Inert Bay had let me down!"

Back on the *Seamoat,* after we'd delivered Tommy back to his wife, Jim became serious again. "They're a mad bunch all right. But what other kind of men could you get to live out here for six months at a time, working in these rain forests without women, getting killed or maimed by the trees? They're not men, they're apes. Most of 'em can't read or write, and many should be in jail. In the old days they often had a choice – work somewhere like this or go to jail. A lot of that blood is still around."

"Tommy's got a real down on Indians," I said.

"Yeah, but he's wrong. It's true some of 'em drink lousy, and are degenerate, but it's not really their fault. For years we shut 'em off in reservations and ignored them. After the war we got a guilty conscience and smothered them with welfare handouts, but all that did was sap their pride – their responsibility."

He sighed. I hadn't heard him talk like this before. "I feel for the Indians," he went on, rubbing his nose. "They weren't born like us to eight-hour days and five-day weeks, to bank accounts, mortgages, and a new car now and again. They were born to real freedom – to fish when they felt like it or when the fish were running, to sit and talk for days, to take off up north after the caribou in their hunting lands, to eat and drink and feast when the time seemed right. Today they still *think* that way, and if they feel that way in the middle of some boring job the white man wants done for a few bucks, well too bad. He'd better go and find someone else."

He opened a can of milk and poured some into the coffee I'd brewed. "Of course, now the government realises a lot of this, and today young Indians are being educated to grow up like other Canadians. But it's a pity, really, because fifty years will see the end of the Indians as a … what's that word? … ethnic … as an ethnic group. Same with the Eskimos."

He stared moodily at the *Seamoat's* black engine block, protruding through the floor. "Tell me," he said, "what do you think of those guys, that crazy lot up there?"

"Not really sure," I replied. "When you're younger, you think fighting and winning means something. Then one day you realise it doesn't."

"They reckon a good brawl clears the air."

"Not so sure about that. A man might fear you if you lick him, but he won't *like* you or change his ideas. And if you can't achieve either, what's the point?"

"Yeah," said Jim thoughtfully, "you may have something there." Then he laughed suddenly, went to the cash box, and took out his .38 revolver. He checked its full magazine and spring, set the safety catch, and put the gun under his pillow. "I wouldn't rely on telling that to the guys around here," he said, "so I'll have this ready, just in case! Two years back a big blonde broad who ran a collector got taken for 1,600 bucks when two guys took her to a dance. One of 'em sneaked back and got into the cash box. Another skipper got beaten over the head for 5,000 bucks up here. I'm not taking chances in Inert Bay."

That night I woke up after two hours' sleep, because in my dream I was still right in the middle of that beer parlour brawl. I lay awake a long time, listening to Jim's heavy snores. I knew then that this wasn't the simple life I wanted either. All the past month had really done was shake the cobwebs from a jaded soul.

Several days later, as we unloaded our third consignment of salmon at Campbell River, I left the boat. Jim's fiancée was flying up from Vancouver to join him for two weeks' holiday. I felt three was a crowd. I didn't want to be with a happy couple, day and night, on a small boat, as it would only drive it home to me that during the long hard winter ahead I was to be alone in the wilds, writing my new novel.

—

During the year that followed I leased a small, isolated plot of land on a cliff top overlooking the Pacific, and with the aid of an extraordinary backwoods log craftsman called Ed Louette I built a small log cabin there. I replaced the old Pontiac with an old milk truck that was square and ugly, but which was far more stable on the forest tracks, and could carry many more materials, not to mention a white spirit cooker and a comfortable bed. I also acquired a new companion – a stray wild dog I called Booto, who had turned up, starving hungry, at the cabin one stormy February night as I was working on my book and loneliness was threatening to overwhelm me. All these events, and my adventures with grizzly bears, bald eagles and killer whales, were fully described in my book *Alone In The Wilderness*, so don't bear repeating here.

4

With the Lusty Men of the Wild Forests

From behind the firs and cedars around the clearing where I was making hasty repairs to my battered old milk truck – my one remaining link with civilisation – there came the strange, rhythmic thudding of a big engine. I looked up with alarm. I had been working on my novel for six months in the little log cabin I'd built in the wilds a hundred miles north of Vancouver, and in all that time I'd not had a single visitor. Not surprising, really, for no ordinary vehicle could get down the tortuous trail I'd hacked through the forest from the old logging tracks above. Angrily, I thought some new logging company must have begun work in the area.

Suddenly, from behind the trees emerged an ugly, grey truck, exactly like mine. From it stepped a huge, square man, whose bright scarlet braces seemed hardly able to hold his huge, powerful form down into a pair of vast blue jeans. A wide grin split his cherubic face into two, like a Hallowe'en pumpkin, and in each hand he held a twelve-pack of potent beer.

It was George Tocher, known to everyone as 'Geordie'. "Hi Mike," he said, flicking off the top of one bottle against the top of another, and handing me one. "Figured you'd had enough of isolation by now, so just came up to terrorise you for a while!"

To be 'terrorised' (western Canadian slang for a hard-drinking visit) by a man like Geordie Tocher was a privilege. I had first met him when I arrived in Vancouver from Britain, and he was the best of those beer parlour pals who had introduced me to Big Jim Olsen, and that memorable fishing adventure with the lusty men of the salmon. I had met Geordie only twice more after that, both times on my shopping trips to Vancouver, but I'd seen enough to know he was a unique character. In booming British Columbia, then the last wild, free-wheeling, free-booting frontier left in the English-speaking hemisphere, there were many rugged entrepreneurs who made, and lost, fortunes overnight. But I knew none quite so free or so wheeling as Geordie. At 42, he was not only a top-flight tree-topper (he could shin his 245 pounds with a life rope up and down 200-foot trees like a monkey) but also a qualified small plane pilot, blaster, scuba diver, boat salvage expert, bulldozer driver and adventure tour bus driver.

Geordie would no sooner work one project up into a success than he'd get bored and start another. Once, when driving to a tree-felling contract near the Yukon border, he filled his truck with cheap second-hand suits from charity shops to sell to the loggers for their hedonistic forays into town. He made as much from the suits as he did from dropping the trees. He always had a wad of money, but never saved any. Harassed men in dark suits were always arriving at his parents' wooden bungalow outside Vancouver, armed with writs, attachments, legal documents and proof-of-delivery letters. They all seemed to know him well, and after he had explained that he wouldn't be sleeping in a dilapidated bus in the back-yard if he had any money, they usually went away smiling – even if not always in a fit state to drive their cars.

I knew I wouldn't get any more work done on the truck, or on my novel, for the rest of that day. What I did *not* know was that I wouldn't do any more work on either for the next two months.

Politely, Geordie examined my little cabin, but it was not until he saw the big log staircase I'd made up the 30-foot cliff that he showed any interest. This had been a fluke – beginner's luck. There had already been one large tree bridging the top of the cliff with the beach, but I'd had to fall a second tree, a seventy-foot fir, which grew some twenty-five yards back from the cliff top. First cutting showed it wanted to fall to the left. Somehow, in a complicated operation with the power saw, sledge hammer and wedges, I managed to drop it exactly side by side with the previous tree so that their trunks were just three inches apart all the way down. When I had cut steps across both trunks I had an ideal staircase to the beach below. What was more, the top of the second tree had snapped off dead in line with the bottom of the first tree.

"Holy crow!" said Geordie when I had explained the operation. "A master faller with twenty years' experience couldn't have done it better. I'm gonna give you a job, you lucky English prick." Short of money as ever, I soon took him up on the offer.

Our first task was a three-week contract to blow up old giant stumps along the route of a new road to the Simon Fraser University on the edge of Vancouver. Some of the fir and cedar stumps were twelve feet high and eight feet across the butt. Geordie had landed the contract by undercutting his rivals. "Usually we charge so much per stump, but my estimate's based on the kind of dynamite we'll use," he explained. "Most blasters today use powerful stuff like Amex or Forsite, which is about 40 per cent nitroglycerine. But a lot of these stumps are so punky we can get away with ordinary stumping powder, which is only 20 per cent." There were nearly 400 stumps, and at a profit of nine dollars a stump we were more than making hay.

My job as assistant blaster was to take a crowbar and a thin shovel, seek under the root clusters, and dig a small tunnel under the stump's centre. Into the hole Geordie placed the dynamite sticks – one for each inch of the stump's diameter. Then he'd crimp on a length of fuse, insert the little explosive cap into the last stick, and tamp the earth back down over the hole. Then he'd light the fuse, and we'd retire behind a large rock. With a great 'Whoomph!' the charge would go off, and the huge stumps would split apart like giant roses, with acrid-smelling smoke drifting up between the great 'petals'.

I was happily tamping down earth with my heel on one large charge of dynamite when Geordie noticed, and let out a yell. "Don't ever let in gravel when you're tamping down," he cried, "it can cause a spark, and goodbye to you, novel and all! And tamp it down with a piece of wood, not your foot!"

Sometimes, for variety, we would load two or three stumps at once, link them all to a twist-grip generator, and trail out some five hundred feet of wire. Then, standing behind something solid, one of us would twist the grip to make the spark at the end of the wire, and up they would all go. It was infinitely satisfying to watch those vast stumps, which had stood there since the early logging days of the early 1890s, split apart like flowers, ready for the big orange 'dozers' to extract them, like rotten teeth, from the mouth of the earth.

On the third day Geordie, who was getting bored again, came over with his big melon grin and a large round boulder in his hands. He looked round carefully for a while, then, seeing no-one, he placed it over one of the stump holes we had loaded and plugged. "Watch this!" he said. "This'll show you the power of the stuff we're using."

He came back to where I was hiding behind a large rock, and handed me the generator. I twisted the handle, and amid the roar and flying debris we saw the rock take off into the air like a great cannonball and land almost a quarter of a mile away in a dense tangle of large fir trees. There was a distant yell, and we saw a shirt-sleeved man emerge, pale-faced, from the brush. Adopting attack as the easiest method of defence, Geordie loudly demanded what the man was doing there. He was not a site worker, and why hadn't he heard Geordie shout "Fire!"? (He hadn't, of course – he had, as usual, yelled the golfer's "Fore!")

But the man, although shaken, wasn't at all angry. Hastily, and guilt-ily, he shouted, "I'm sorry, boys. Real sorry. Guess I lost my way." And we saw him creep back into the bush, pick up what looked like a rifle, and sneak away. It was not the hunting season, and clearly there was one intrepid 'hunter' who wouldn't chance his luck again until it was.

We were not working alone all the time. There was a man called Greg, who was a sort of truck-driving foreman who walked about with a pronounced limp. He had a whistle, and a board with papers clipped to it. He was a pal of Geordie, and had helped him get not only this contract but also our next job, which was a three-week tree-felling engagement further north. Greg was a good name for him, because he looked a little like Gregory Peck, except that he sported a droopy moustache and his eyes were a bit too close together.

Then there was Fred Jackson, who drove the big D9 'Cat' bulldozer. Whenever we came to a big, newish stump that wouldn't blow easily, and our normal tamping over the loaded hole wasn't enough, Fred would rumble up with his big Cat and backpile earth and other debris on top of the charge before we blew it.

I liked Fred because he was total – total *anti*. He was about 55 and had a profile like a Scottie dog. Thick cleavages round his wide mouth gave a saturnine cast to his countenance in a way that made the late Humphrey Bogart look effeminate. He was tall and skinny, and far stronger than he looked. In beer parlours Fred would find himself among a bunch of 'rangitan' loggers (derived from orang-utan – the ape!) fresh from the woods, and he would watch with polite interest as they gambled on the arm-wrestling. When invited to try his luck he'd quietly bet the winner twenty bucks he couldn't beat him. Fred never put anyone's arm down, it is true, but no-one put his down either. He had an odd way of locking his arm that no-one could move. And he'd win his bet, because he'd bet the other couldn't *beat* him.

"Aw, I just got freak joints," he'd grin, as he scooped the wad of notes off the table. Once Geordie asked Fred how his wife was. "Oh, she's okay," he replied gruffly. "I slung a coupla chunks of raw meat into her cage after I got up. She's fine now!"

Fred took a lot of knowing, for on first meeting he appeared down-right unfriendly. He would acknowledge introductions with a curt nod, and if he deigned to shake your hand at all, he'd seize the tips of your fingers at the last second in a vice-like grip. Some said he was mean because he came from the prairies of Alberta, and resented the British Columbian men's predilection for naming prairie men 'flatlanders' or 'stubble jumpers'.

We were talking with Fred once about crowded city life, and neigh-bourliness in general, and about how good it was to be working in the great outdoors. "Yeah," growled Fred, who owned some twenty-five acres on the coast. "Out here, if you can't love your neighbour, you've got room enough to leave the goddam bastard alone!" But Fred could perform wonders with his big Cat, and sometimes I'd see Greg watching him at work with a sort of envy, and wonder why.

It was on our tenth day that we blew up the dog.

We were working alone at the time, and we had just loaded up the last stump and lit a one-minute fuse, when an aggressive little terrier ran into the clearing, barking and yapping. It saw the fuse fizzing away, and promptly dived into the top of the hole and burrowed after it.

"Holy crow!" cried Geordie. "That's Fred's dog. Hey, Spot, get out of there, you little ****!" He waved his arms frantically, but to no avail. Suddenly the charge went off. We watched, mesmerised, as the little dog shot up into the air, described a very slow, double-looping parabola, and hurtled down again, to land with a sickening thud on the ground.

We walked over. Sadly Geordie picked up the little body by the tail and shook it gently, but it was clearly as dead as a doornail. "Oh hell," Geordie said, "we'd better get out of here before Fred comes along. He's an 'ornery character at the best of times." He hurled the dog on top of a huge brushpile that was to be lit the next damp day, and we left.

Later, as we had a drink with Greg in the local beer parlour, Geordie seemed unusually quiet. It was here I learned that Greg had acquired his limp through an odd accident while driving a bulldozer, two winters back, on a snow-covered mountain above Vancouver. Every time he drove his 'Cat' up the mountain he'd had a problem turning it round to go down again, thanks to its natural propensity to skid sideways. So he had hit on the idea of hitching the tracks round a stump, edging round it until he'd got the machine in line again to go down the mountain. Unfortunately, on one turn a stump had broken off clean, the parallel cleats on the 'dozer tracks had acted as miniature skis, and thirty tons of bulldozer had hurtled down the mountain side with poor Gregory aboard. On its first somersault it had thrown him off and snapped his thigh bone.

"And I wasn't even drunk," he added miserably. It seemed clear that Greg had a penchant for trouble, although it was more than matched by his ability to get out of trouble again.

"I heard you were had up a few weeks back for drivin' an overloaded trailer?" said Geordie suddenly.

Greg sighed. "Yeah. Had too many logs aboard, tryin' to save a double journey. The load was over the ten-foot limit."

"What happened?"

"Oh, I got off okay," said Greg laconically. "Y'see, I found out it would have been okay if the load had been *fodder* and not logs. So I got this goat, starved it for three days and took it along to the court with a maple log. When the magistrate says he doesn't believe my load was fodder, in comes the goat and starts eatin' the bark off the log! Everyone on the court fell about, and I got off!"

At this Geordie and I burst into hearty guffaws, but Geordie soon relapsed into gloom again. The dead dog was too much on his mind. Presently he excused himself, and came back with a couple of bottles of rye he'd bought at a nearby liquor store. "Come on," he said, "we got to go and tell Fred about his damn dog."

We went to see Fred in his trailer. We flourished the rye, drank and talked, and talked and drank, and when Fred had a good few inside him and was feeling happy Geordie gently broke the news.

There was a silence. Fred tapped his leathery fingers on the table in a devilishly scary tattoo, then drew a deep breath. "Oh well, it can't be helped," he said philosophically. "Forget it, boys. He always was a yappy little bastard anyway!"

A few minutes later there was a scratching noise at the door. When Fred opened it, there stood Spot – bedraggled and dazed, but still very much alive. He hadn't been killed – only stunned. "You should have listened to his *heartbeat,* you drunken bum," said Fred, with a happy grin – the first I'd seen on that lugubrious face.

In my forty-four years I had seen most of the world, but I never met a bunch of men more colourful than those in the British Columbia bush. Although they came from a dozen different countries, they all had one thing in common – to work hard in the western world's last free frontier, to enjoy life while freeing its vast plethora of natural resources, and maybe, but usually as a side issue, to get rich. The log, fish and mining camps all had a rangy, zestful outdoors aura, like some huge wacky army of keen, hairy rookies, who went about their work and play with enormous elan and physical gusto. Many of them had several skills at their fingertips, and small groups of friends could 'cruise' the entire country for jobs together. When the blasting job was completed, Fred, Greg, Geordie and I were all employed on the tree-falling contract a couple of hundred miles further north. On our first night there – a Friday – we were invited in the beer parlour to attend a local wedding the next day.

We were driving there in Geordie's truck when I said "There's something burning" to Greg, who was sitting next to me. He sniffed around the jolting, bouncing truck. "Can't smell a thing." A few seconds later he yelled "Goddammit, you're right. Stop the truck!"

Geordie braked, and Greg leaped out. The entire crotch of his trousers was smouldering from the embers of the pipe he'd stuffed into his pocket. Dancing like a marionette, he grabbed a bottle of beer and doused the fire.

No-one seemed to mind that he attended both the wedding and the reception with beer-soaked, scorched trousers, but that wasn't surprising. The reception was held in a ramshackle 'community' hall, and to get to it we had to wade through mud a foot deep. Outside, the girls all took their shoes off and rinsed their muddy feet in buckets of brown water. The reception slowly turned into a wild, noisy barn dance, and that night Greg seemed a favourite among the local women, who stared as much at his midriff as at his surly, handsome face. I thought any moment the Mounties would enter and arrest him for indecent exposure!

Despite such moments, the actual tree-falling work was hard and dangerous, especially for a virtual beginner like myself. Although a top faller could earn ninety bucks a day, especially if he was a high rigger (who climbs and tops the tallest trees before falling them), I wasn't in that class. It was just as well we had only to fall the trees and buck them to the required length, then move on. Behind us came the limbers – the youngsters who set choker wires round the butts – and the 'Cat' drivers who winched and yarded the logs out and along the skid roads. I worked alone with Geordie, falling the trees in the direction he told me.

It was exhausting at first. A man could get tired in that rugged terrain clambering over fallen trunks just carrying his lunch, never mind a forty-five-pound power saw. If you heard your companion's tree fall and his saw didn't start up again, you went to see what was wrong. He could have been hit by a butt that bounced back, or split into a 'barber's chair' and crushed him; or he could have been struck by a 'widow maker' (a falling branch). But even here, although Geordie was well within safety limits, he would fool about. Sometimes he would cut through four or five trees at various strategic spots, then fall the last one so it hit the next, which hit the next, and so on, so that the whole lot crashed down through the forest like a series of giant dominoes.

On our fourth night we met an old Swedish faller called Muskrat Pete – so called because he often carried a cane for whacking muskrats. Muskrat worked at the highest point of the forest, and he'd been having trouble with a hungry and over-friendly black bear. He first discovered the young sow tucking into his lunch sandwiches, which he'd left in a hollow log. "I'll fix her," he swore. Next day he made some 'snoose' sandwiches, with tobacco from crushed old cigarette butts between the bread. Naturally, he was enraged to find that the bear happily devoured them too, enjoying every bite of the awful meal.

Muskrat was another wild character. For seven years he had been a tugboat skipper, plying the Pacific coast of British Columbia, towing log booms down to the Vancouver mills. Two incidents had finally lost him the job, forcing him back to his old trade as a faller. The first was when a young mate on watch at night had let the scow they were towing run up on a sandbank at low tide, after having assured Pete he was far from tired. Muskrat was furious when a vacationing official of his company, who witnessed the crunch, phoned head office and sent for another tug to tow them off. Muskrat had spurned such help, making the newly arrived tug wait idly by while he set an anchor behind a rocky spur and *winched* the scow off at high tide without help.

The second incident proved the last straw to his employers. One evening Pete had lost three sections of his log boom when going through the treacherous rapids near Stuart Island, and he informed his head office over the public radio phone. A young and inexperienced official, who didn't want it on *his* head that so many logs had been lost to the licensed log beachcombers, told Muskrat to go back and retrieve the lost sections. Muskrat knew well enough that the sections would be breaking up, and that if he tried it he would as likely as not lose the entire boom. They argued, and then Muskrat lost his temper and yelled at the head office official over the radio, "You know what you can do with your tugboat. Stick it right up your ★★★★!" Immediately the Vancouver phone operator cut him off, and berated him for using such language over the public radio phone for everyone to hear. Muskrat was quickly apologetic, said he'd forgotten he was on the public phone, and begged her to *please* reconnect him. As she did so, Muskrat bellowed down the phone, "And that goes for your ✱✱✱✱ log booms too!"

Canadians are insulted if you suggest they are basically a nation of ex-domestic servants who fled the Old Country in search of a better life. It hurts, too, because there is an *element* of truth in the saying. It is perhaps an inherited desire to escape this labourer/domestic servant/crofter background that makes many Canadian pioneers, especially the rugged BC men, such colourful and thoroughly independent rebels. They hate to be classed as 'employees', and apart from possessing several skills, many have their fingers in several pies. Fred Jackson, for instance, had a half share in a garage and gas station on the coast, and he worked in it most of the winters.

Like most outpost garages, Fred's would become a meeting place for dedicated imbibers from the beer parlours. I was there once when Fred had just recovered from a minor operation. The continual onslaught of broken down old crocks to repair, which most of the loggers and fishermen drove, was proving a little too much for him. And when a tourist behaved too high-handedly, and one of the pumps suddenly went haywire, Fred cursed loudly, and for a few seconds the air seemed full of wrenches and tyre levers ricochetting from the floors and walls. A group of drinkers, quite used to such outbursts, just leaped outside and carried on drinking.

At the end of our first week of tree falling, a small man with bushy eyebrows headed towards our beer parlour table. Geordie groaned at Fred and Greg, rolling his eyes upwards, and then smiled. "Hi, Lloyd," he said, as he dodged Lloyd's playful grab at his scalp; "you're just in time for the next round! Thought you'd run out of places to run!"

Lloyd frowned in mock fury. "If you had somethin' to back it up with, Geordie" (who was three times his size), "I'd invite ya outside!"

"You want to strap on your guns or just chew some gravel?" growled Geordie. "Siddown and get out your dough!" Lloyd sat down, and as small men often do, dominated most of the talk that night.

I couldn't quite understand Geordie's initial faint antagonism. For a week Lloyd seemed the epitome of the ideal general logger. He waltzed round with the crew behind us, limbing and bucking up the trees, setting chokers, piling the brush for burning, and carrying old motor oil and tyres to help the huge fires burn.

"You'll see," said Geordie cryptically. "I'm just wonderin' what trick he'll pull *this* time."

Halfway through our third week we found out. Lloyd climbed up one huge brush pile, treading skilfully from one fir branch to another, tipped out a large can of oil at the top, and then gave a loud yell as he appeared to lose his footing. Down he went, tumbling, twisting and yelling, and landed in a crumpled heap at the bottom. "He's done it again," sighed Geordie, not even going over to see how Lloyd was. The crew members picked up Lloyd's groaning form and carried him to the bunkhouse.

It was now that Geordie explained. Lloyd and hard work were just incompatible. He would get himself a job, work like crazy for about ten days, winning the confidence of employers and crew alike, and then stage a spectacular 'accident'. This put him on full worker's compensation for at least a couple of weeks while he 'recovered'. As this worked out at about fifteen dollars a week, and with chow and lodging free and beer at fourteen cents a glass, all Lloyd really needed to do to live nice and easy for much of the time was maintain his acrobatic techniques!

It was at the end of our tree-falling contract – when I'd escaped with no more injury than skinned knuckles, bruised ribs, and a couple of blue-black toes where a log had dropped on my foot – that I almost became a gold miner. In the beer parlour on our last half day, Saturday, Geordie introduced me to a couple of new faces, Sandy and his partner Lorne, who were blasting out an old gold mine. After a long sales pitch about the vast nuggets still left in the old seam, they invited me into a prospecting partnership with them. It would cost me only a few hundred dollars, they explained, and I was interested enough to go and view their operation.

They took great pains to explain how they blew the rock out and sieved the rubble through their sluice boxes in a nearby creek. But two things put me off. One was their obvious addiction to alcohol, which seemed to cut overmuch into their working day. The other was that I couldn't fathom why, if they were doing so well, they needed such a greenhorn partner. Next day, while I was toying with the idea of staying with them, Geordie put me wise, as he had made some enquiries. Sandy and Lorne had been happily blowing out the rock and finding gold dust and small nuggets, but had failed to notice they were on the side of a mountain gorge, at the bottom of which ran a single-track railway line. Some of their falling rocks had damaged the line, and after a posse of Mounties had ridden up and told them to get the hell out, they learned that restitution would amount to a small matter of some $8,000, but in a month they'd only found gold worth some $7,700. It had been raining heavily for two days, and I decided I wasn't cut out for gold mining – or for being 'panhandled', either!

We were on the point of leaving camp when Greg came up. He said he'd been on the phone, and that he'd got a week's work on Whistler Mountain above Vancouver, driving a snow plough at the start of the ski season. Would we care to go along for a few days? Geordie looked at me. "Looks like we're going skiing!" he said. "Sure, Greg, we *deserve* a vacation!"

We drove down to Whistler, and for a few days enjoyed the skiing despite my being a novice – until Greg's snow plough broke down. It hadn't moved in over an hour, and a group of skiers and happy imbibers from the ski lodge had assembled round it. We hiked over and found Greg down in a deep pit in the snow, trying to repair something underneath the plough. It was taking some time to fix, partly because the members of the group kept handing down flagons of cheap wine for Greg to sip, along with their advice. Geordie climbed up on the plough and, to Greg's shouted instructions, started and re-started the engine, enveloping poor Greg in clouds of black smoke.

After half an hour of this we saw Greg suddenly stagger and collapse in the pit, and a couple of other men who'd been leaning over also looked very groggy. It was clear Greg had been overcome by the carbon monoxide fumes from the engine. We hauled him out, and as we laid him on the snow I said to Geordie, "You'd better give him mouth-to-mouth respiration, Geordie. You've done first aid."

"Not me," he replied hastily. "When I do that I always get personally involved!" Another man looked down at Greg, who was rather pale, and said, "Gee, he doesn't appeal to me either." So we hauled Greg groggily back onto his feet and walked him about the snowy mountain until he came to. Geordie expressed the opinion that Greg ought to go back to

37

his apartment in the city for the rest of the day. Greg agreed, shaking his head violently. "Gee, that wine – it sure has a kick!" he said. We stood him on his skis, pointed him in the direction of his truck and Vancouver, and launched him towards home.

Two days later we were in a small café, back on the wild coast where I had my little cabin. I thought I was at the end of my lusty adventures with Geordie, and was now looking forward to my peaceful life with just the wild birds, animals and fish in my little paradise, tackling the hardest section of my novel, which still lay ahead. But it was not to be. I still had another strange day and night before me. The cafe owner was clearing some land nearby for a trailer site. He had a rented tractor for just one more day, and he offered us a hundred dollars if we would pile and burn all the brush left by the clearing operation.

"Sure," said Geordie without consulting me; "I need an oil change anyway!" Down at the local garage we changed the oil in his truck, and mine, and carried the old oil and some used tyres to the site. We piled up the brush with the tractor, emptied the oil containers over the brush and tyres, and by evening we had four huge piles burning away merrily. As we sat in the beer parlour that night, resting from our labours and making liquid incursions into the extra fifty bucks apiece, a waiter came up in a hurry and summoned Geordie. A local cabin owner, worried about the sparks floating about near his premises, had contacted the beer parlour to try and find the brush burners before contacting the fire brigade in the small town seventeen miles to the south. (Under BC law brush burners near residential districts have to guard their fires overnight.)

We hurried round, and Geordie placated the cabin owner by promising to watch the fires personally all night, and that he'd have free firewood from the cafe owner throughout the winter. We spent the rest of the night fire-watching from our trucks, with a small fire of our own, on which we barbecued Polish sausage, and mulled wine with cloves and cinnamon from the cafe.

Next day, as our two trucks lurched down the winding rocky track through the forests to my cliff-top cabin above the Pacific, I was dog tired, and looking forward to the months of peaceful isolation and writing ahead. But we had gone only a few hundred yards when Geordie sounded his horn and stopped. When I got to him he was out of his truck and gazing with apparent rapture at the burnt-out shell of an old cabin in the trees.

"Look at that!" he exclaimed.

"Yes, it's been there since 1920," I said, following his gaze. "The man who built it brought a box of dynamite in by the stove, because he heard it was dangerous when it got wet. He went for stores, and when he got back …" I indicated the shattered wreck. I expected Geordie to guffaw at this odd but true tale, but he didn't. He just stood staring, lost in delight. "Not the cabin," he said; "the *biffy*! Just look at that beautiful outhouse!" I followed his gaze towards a small, shed-like contraption hidden behind some bushes near a cedar tree.

We walked over to it. Geordie admired its golden cedar shake roof, and then opened the door. It was a twin-holer, and it spoke deeply of intimacy. The very air of this ancient woodland loo was redolent of unusual harmony and a rare domestic bliss. Geordie stepped back with a loving look on his face.

"You know something?" he said. "People talk together, dance together, sleep together, make love together but they never shi…. Holy Crow. I just got an idea. I'm goin' to take it back to Vancouver and hold a biffy party up Hollyburn mountain! Help me move it!"

He went back to his truck, and returned with ropes, blocks and pulleys. We finally managed to strap the outhouse onto the back of his vehicle.

"Now this will really be a party with a difference," said Geordie breathlessly. "A biffy, you see, is basic, elemental, primeval, and takes a man back to the old pioneering days. We'll truck all those little office secretaries back in Vancouver up Hollyburn and let 'em all look back at their little high-rise nests from the throne of a real old biffy. Maybe get an old piano up there too!"

He climbed up into the driving seat and started the engine. "Besides," he added with unanswerable, unassailable logic, "I never stole a biffy before."

My last sight of Geordie Tocher for nearly a year was of him carefully driving both truck and biffy up the precipitous track, looking back anxiously now and again in case its little shake roof got damaged by the trees. It seemed a fitting end to that year's adventures with the lusty men of the wild forests.

5

With Booto (And Stars) in Hollywood

When my second winter in the Canadian wilds was looming, I realised I was getting desperately short of money, and with fish and seafood harder to catch in the colder weather I would need to spend more on food in the local store. The money I had earned in short jobs as salmon fisherman, logger and assistant blaster had long gone; so had most of the money I'd gained by selling off my only life insurance policy. I had been turned down for jobs by two Vancouver editors, who wanted younger journalists who knew the country and area well, not a dishevelled-looking British hermit.

I was still faintly remembered in the world of celebrity journalism, and although the film Mecca of Hollywood lay 1,382 miles to the south, it seemed I had no other choice. I would go back there, tour the movie studios, interview all the major stars I could get to, and sell the stories to my old magazines in half a dozen countries. What I now needed most was a *cheap* place to live. Accordingly, I drove down to Vancouver and bought new tools, timber and materials to make a better 'trailer home' in the back of my old square milk truck, so that if things became tough in Hollywood I could at least live in it. Then I rattled back to the wild coast and Booto.

But as I built my new 'home' into its cavernous interior, and prepared for the onslaught on Hollywood, I felt I must leave Booto behind. It was a hard decision, but he had spent his life on that rugged coast, a wild creature who loved to run free. He often left me to go and visit old friends anyway, and it would be cruel to expose him to the perils and confines of smog-ridden big-city life in Los Angeles, or leave him cooped up in the hot truck when I visited studios. I also intended to tour Mexico, and with little money and no sponsors I would have more than enough problems getting through the US and Mexican borders on my *own*. I arranged for Booto to be fed by Fred Jackson and his wife, and also by Stanley Dimopolous, the owner of a cafe up the road, whose children Booto loved to visit.

On the day I left, Booto watched me pack the truck with reproach in his eyes, and whined moodily as he saw my belongings being stacked inside it. Then he disappeared. I thought he had realised he'd better go back to Fred's or to the cafe. As I drove up to the store to stock up with food and drink for the trip I saw him from the corner of my eye, lying in the cafe's forecourt, but I didn't trust myself to look at him directly. On the way back he was no longer there; it made it easier, somehow, not having a last sight of him.

I drove on towards the ferry, fifty miles to the south, but in a bend of the road way past the track to our cabin I saw him trotting along. He looked like he always did on the road, padding slightly sideways as if his back feet were trying to overtake his front, like a little brown bear from the back.

He heard the truck coming and turned round, but I went straight past him, feeling awful – but I didn't dare stop. In the mirror I saw him start to run, tearing after the truck, leaning over sideways round the bend like a speedway rider as he desperately tried to catch up. I trod hard on the accelerator and went round many more bends until I'd lost him, but after a mile I had to stop, as tears made it impossible for me to see the road clearly any more. I pulled into a small clearing in an agony of indecision. All the memories of the first long, hard winter when he'd been my only companion came back – the way he always came and put his head on my knee when I was troubled. I didn't want to leave him, but how could I take him?

There was a mad scraping swirl of stones by the truck's door and there he was. Even in his panting, exhausted state his ears were pricked forward, his eyes full of questioning pain – why are you leaving me?

"Oh, come on then, you daft old fool," was all I could say as I slammed the door behind him. Booto leaped onto the bench seat, covered my face with licks, and then dived onto the floor behind and curled up out of sight, in case I changed my mind. Then we set off on the long drive to Hollywood.

Surprisingly, we had no trouble at the American border. Although I stopped at a Vancouver vet's and had Booto suitably jabbed, dosed and legally certificated, the border police at Blaine didn't ask a single question about him. All they did was remove my potatoes and lemons and wave us on our way.

We rumbled down Route 99 through Seattle, Portland and Eugene, and the soft folds in the hills of Oregon near Oakland looked at first like those in Devon, England. They folded away like a green velvet curtain thrown to the ground by the hand of God, and as the sun shone on it grey rock strata appeared: some birch woods glowed silver, but other folds were in near darkness.

We made the mistake of spending the first night in an official rest area near Roseberg, where we found that American truck drivers seemed never to turn off their engines, perhaps because there was so much cheap gas around, or maybe they were just too tired to throw the switch. They came within mere feet of the truck and left their engines thudding away while they went for a snack or a leak!

On the first day Booto was sick, but by the end of the second day he had found his 'truck legs' and happily snapped at flies and wasps. He loved killing wasps, and whenever we stopped to cook up on the little white spirit stove, any meat-hunting wasp soon found itself clopped to death in Booto's jaws, shaken fast into the ground and rubbed into the dust by a hefty paw. After a morning fill-up outside Roseberg I was perplexed by the first truck weigh station. Was I a van or a truck? I stopped at the station, but they just laughed at me and waved me on.

As we rumbled on, skirting the town of Grants Pass, the land beneath the mountain opened into a great valley surrounded by high hills. Higher up we were hit by hailstorms and stones one minute and blinding sunshine the next, interspersed with drifting skirts of grey rain. Past the Klamath Falls a large snow zone was posted and the first orange sandstone mountains appeared, flecked with scrubby green pines, and we hit the California border at a small place called Hilt at 11.45 am. The usual border inspection for plants occurred, and again my (new) oranges and lemons were taken. Through towns with names like Drain, Yreka and Weed we drove, and then the huge form of the 14,162-foot Mount Shasta loomed on our left, looking like an upturned ice cream cone, perfectly conical.

Once I saw a sign telling motorists to watch out for falling rocks – and I spied a man on a lower summit hurling a few smallish ones down! Was he doing it to satisfy the tourists? We reached the Shasta Lake recreation area at 3 pm, spent forty minutes on lunch, and were rattling through Sacramento by 7 pm. Here the land was flat and agricultural, with distant mountains all around. We camped for the night in an orange grove behind Livingstone near Modesto, well away from any 'recreation areas'. Even so, the traffic ran all night along the nearby main road: it sounded as though vehicles were about to go through us, but no-one actually bothered us.

We struck camp and left at 8.43 am with 289 miles to go to Los Angeles city. I'd had a slight gut upset during the night, but three breakfast eggs bound me up well enough. Although my old van could not be teased over 55 mph we filled up again just past Bakersfield, crossed the LA county line at 1 pm and the LA city limit at 2.15 pm. I counted eleven dead cats on the road that day. I'm not fond of domestic cats, but I felt some department should have cleaned them up! I made straight for the Hollywood area, bought a map, and located a large green area called Griffith Park, which had many leafy, grassy and hilly patches. For the first two nights that's where we camped 'wild'.

I had three main priorities before I could start work: get an apartment, get a phone, and get necessary accreditation. The apartment sort of fell into my lap as I was strolling up Cherokee Avenue, just off Hollywod Boulevard. A man stepped out of Burlington Mansions and said that if I was looking for somewhere to live, his block was not only reasonable, but if I guaranteed to stay at least three months the first month would be free! So Booto and I moved into what was just a cheap room with a small kitchen/shower unit and a bed that could be slammed upwards against the wall every morning, to save space. A man at the first private telephone company I rang said he would be round in a couple of hours. He was, and in return for a small deposit and a signed receipt he plugged in my new phone. I then hiked to the head office of the Academy for Motion Picture Arts And Sciences, which runs the annual Oscars ceremony and much of Hollywood's film business, and met the woman in charge of foreign correspondents' accreditations. She looked through my sheaf of letters from the editors of top magazines in half a dozen countries, saying they would welcome stories from me, and gave me the necessary certificate I needed to gain entry to the major studios. She was a very attractive middle-aged lady called Irene, and she readily accepted my invitation to lunch, during which she gave me many useful tips on dealing with studio publicity chiefs.

What now surprised me most was how Booto took Hollywood in his stride. Maybe the wonderful range of new food smells as we hiked the boulevards helped sustain his spirits. He learnt kerb drill in two days, stopping at main roads, walking over pedestrian crossings, and keeping to heel when I told him. He waited patiently on his first-ever lead outside supermarkets and the Hollywood Post Office – which became our lifeline to our small income.

Our home apartment block was a haven for transients, hopeful actors waiting alone by telephones, and minority groups – including dogs. A pal of mine from London was working temporarily with a group of Mexicans, touring the poorer parts of Los Angeles with cheap family photo deals. One night I was invited to smoke cannabis in one of the Mexicans' rooms, along with my pal. I did smoke, but only a pipe, and I never inhaled the smoke. On being exhorted to inhale the cannabis smoke deeply I made half-hearted attempts to comply, but apart from making me cough it seemed to have no effect on me whatever. I did learn that the best kind of local cannabis was called 'Acapulco gold', but these lads could not afford it. Booto refused to stay in the room, and I soon left too, convinced that cannabis smoking was a waste of both time and money.

Booto's only Hollywood 'hang up' was the elevator. For two weeks he flatly refused to follow me into any lifts. He viewed the whirring cables, unstable floors and clanking metal gates with alarm. Finally I had to drag him in. Then, with all four feet planted wide apart like a landlubber on a pitching ship's deck he crouched, glaring mistrustfully at the moving floor, hating every second of the ride. At the top, when the gates opened, he would charge out through the legs of waiting passengers like a small express train.

Before long people naturally complained, and Booto was banned from the lifts – which suited him just fine. From then on he hurtled up the stairs to our fourth-floor room, pausing on each landing to look back at me with a gleeful tongue-lolling grin that said "There! Isn't this a lot better than that smoky old lift? Use your *legs*, idiot, it's good for you!"

Hollywood is in many ways a dream town, founded on ideas, intangibles, like a carnival that never quite moved on. On one of our morning walks I found Booto staring intently into one of the neat gardens. A man there was solemnly planting big gaudy flowers in the soil – *plastic* flowers! But once I realised that in Hollywood artificiality is part of the reality, it was easier to come to terms with it, and within a few weeks Booto and I became part of the local scene. As I began to sell my interviews with stars my finances swiftly improved.

It was Booto's intelligence that helped us win the tenancy of a beautiful three-roomed cottage in North Gardner Street, Beverley Hills, right next door to where Raymond Burr (star of TV's *Perry Mason* and *Ironside* series) was temporarily living. The cottage stood at the bottom of the elegant garden of a big house, and had its own wooden staircase and a profusion of vines and roses around its door. But the landlord, Mr Schneider, took one look at Booto and reacted with horror.

"I'm sorry," he said. "But we can't have a big dog here. Our garden costs a great deal to keep up, and besides, we had an actor with a dog here before. The darned animal kept us awake half the night with its barking."

As Booto stood looking querulously from one of us to the other, I said, "Booto won't touch your garden, Mr Schneider. In all the time I've known him he's never performed his toilet within fifty yards of the home. What's more, he doesn't bark."

"He doesn't bark?"

"No. Not unless I tell him to. I'll show you." As I walked back to my truck for some dog food, Booto rose splendidly to the occasion. He smiled, wagged his tail, licked Mr Schneider's nervous hand, sat up and begged with his most endearing look, and by the time I got back he and Mr Schneider were solemnly shaking hands.

I held the food out to Booto. "What do you say?" I asked.

"Whuff," he replied softly.

"Louder," I said. "Louder!"

"WOOF!" he barked, shattering the still air.

"Now softly," I said. "Softer."

Booto appeared to purse his lips, making a little 'O' with the front of his mouth, and answered with the merest "Pfff".

When Mr Schneider had finished laughing, he handed me the key. "We have plenty of spare linen if you need any," he said.

For five months the cottage was our base, and sometimes Booto came with me when I interviewed famous stars at studios, on movie locations in deserts or mountains, or at their homes. He seemed singularly unimpressed that the fingers stroking his ruff, patting his head or shaking his paw belonged to such luminaries as Raymond Burr, Robert Mitchum, Dean Martin, Omar Sharif, Rock Hudson, Robert Stack, Anthony Newley, Joan Collins, John Mills, Claudia Cardinale, Patrick McGoohan, Kim Novak, Doris Day or Yvonne de Carlo. And after our life in the wilds of Canada I too felt like an alien from another world at times, as if Booto and I were merely superimposed upon the Hollywood landscape.

Whenever the smog, the trivial talk, the glare of neon and the blare of advertising became too much, we'd take the truck to Griffith Park. There Booto and I pounded on foot through the cool mountains in the moonlight, keeping a little in touch with our reality up north.

Many of the top stars we met were millionaires who occasionally admitted they felt a little trapped by their possessions. Some even had direct burglar alarm lines to the nearest police station, which was rare in the late 1960s. Booto's quaint mannerisms, acquired to beg for scraps in Canada, stood him in good stead in a town that judged its inhabitants largely by their ability to perform in public. At parties he would quickly ingratiate himself with the starlets – probably because he was one of the few males with real character who didn't make personal propositions –

and they would usually lead him to the kitchen, which was further than they took me!

At one celebrity-studded occasion, a private party held high above Hollywood's lights on Doheny Drive, I discovered yet another of Booto's odd quirks that, because I was a pipe smoker, I hadn't seen before: he simply hated lighted cigarette ends. Hearing loud laughter coming from the outdoor patio, I went out and found a group of actors throwing lighted cigarette butts onto the concrete. And Booto was instantly pouncing on them and furiously rubbing them out with his big paws. Such acts often made him the focal point of conversation, and I'd have to tell and re-tell the story of how I'd met him, and something of our primitive lives together in the great outdoors.

Few of the envied top names we met seemed to have found the simple happiness Booto and I had together. Only one, Peter Finch, seemed to truly share our feelings about big-city life. At the time he had a primitive home and estate in the West Indies, where he spent much time with his hands in the earth, planting fruit trees or hoeing vegetables for his own table. Peter compared it all with his temporary sterile life in Beverley Hills, where no-one ever walks, and the big limousines purr up spotless front drives and slide silently under electronic doors that sometimes hide the secret minor tragedies enacted behind the perfect facades.

One quiet night he had gone for a walk alone and there hadn't been a human in sight. "There were all these perfect front lawns with their sprinklers going," he said, "and it could have been a ghost town, devoid of life. Suddenly a brown dog ran up to me, his tail wagging with delight at seeing someone other than himself actually on *foot*. We walked a while together till we came to a garden full of *weeds*. We both went in and rolled on those weeds. To me, it was the most beautiful sight I'd seen since I arrived back here!" The dog, he was astounded to find, was my Booto.

Peter had recently finished the role that elevated him to stardom, playing Farmer Bolwood, hopelessly in love with Julie Christie in *Far From The Madding Crowd*, and he gave me some of his earthy philosophy. "There is something deep in me that says I must get back to basics, to realities. I'm very much aware of fatty degeneration of the brain *and* of the soul. Of course it's nice to earn lots of money from films, as I have heavy responsibilities to my ex-wives and children. But I could beach myself from films at any moment and be just as happy. My ego has all gone, really. The way I live in Jamaica proves that. The place is called Bamboo, and I live there alone and do much of the work on the eight acres of fruit trees and timber myself. When I feel the need for company I go to the village bar two miles away and join my fellow farmers, who are all Jamaicans. I've had the fine homes, fast cars, elegant possessions – now all gone – and that's all I really need socially now." 'Finchy' was a man after my own heart, and he, Booto and I went on several walks together.

As Booto became used to the new neighbourhood he began to sneak off on his own when I was typing for long periods. As he seemed so streetwise I wasn't unduly worried. He usually came back after a few hours, and if he had a relaxed grin on his face I knew some pampered movie town bitch had bestowed her boudoir favours on him. I could imagine him listening with polite gravity to all their big-city neuroses, then smartly rendering his small Casanova service, before figuratively doffing his hat and coming home for his supper.

Once he disappeared overnight. I found him *seven miles* away on the beach at Santa Monica, quietly sniffing a palm tree. He looked at me without surprise, then came over with a big tongue-lolling grin as if to say "Oh hello. Glad you turned up. You can save me that little trot home!" After that I bought him a more expensive, chain-link lead.

At one time he was having a serious romance with a comely Dobermann bitch up in the Hollywood hills, and if I didn't let him out first thing in the morning he would moan and groan and flop about heavily on the floor, deliberately disturbing my desk work. Also, while at the height of his 'affairs', he would snore heavily at night, dream about fighting off other suitors, and make whuffling noises like a shunting train letting off steam. Naturally, all this woke me up, so then I'd wake *him* up, tell him to stop snoring or barking in his sleep, and imitate him so he would understand what he was doing.

That was my big mistake. From then on he knew that snoring and whuffling noises annoyed me, and on the days I wouldn't let him out, he'd lie on the floor as if asleep and snore and whuffle loudly. I finally cottoned on to his trickery when I caught him doing it with his eyes open.

One day he suddenly ran off, pulling his fine new lead from my hand, and ignoring my shout to come back. I was furious, but after a couple of days I became worried. There was a story about vivisectionists in the local paper, and I was afraid Booto's natural friendliness would have him end up on some scientist's operating table. I telephoned the city's dog pounds.

"Yeah," said the official at the biggest pound in downtown Los Angeles. "Sure, we got a big brown dog in here with one floppy ear. We've got hundreds!" I drove to all the pounds, looked into a thousand frightened eyes, but there was no sign of Booto.

On the fourth morning at 3 am I was woken by a scratching and whining at the door. There stood Booto, shivering in the rain, unkempt. His fine new lead had gone, but around his neck was a metal clasp from a much cheaper lead, and some stout cord. Someone had caught him and tied him up, but he had managed to gnaw his way free through the cord. Although he'd had a narrow squeak I scolded him, and gave him a couple of hard slaps. He knew they were coming, of course, and never stopped gulping down his mince and biscuits or wagging his tail throughout.

Booto didn't mind a little punishment if he *knew* he was guilty. He doubtless reasoned that a few whacks across the rump were a small price to pay for amorous dalliance with the delectable damsels of Hollywood. What he hated was being confined in any way. After this escapade I tied him in the garden for a couple of days. He didn't bark or make a noisy fuss but just lay there, his head disconsolate on his white boots, making soulful sheep's eyes at me every time I went past. "You're just jealous anyway," his look seemed to say. Of course, I soon relented, but I tied a plastic disc to his collar with my phone number on it, plus a note asking whoever found him to let me know for a small reward. For ten days he behaved impeccably – probably his lady love was off heat. He trotted along the Beverly Hills sidewalks, waited for me at corners, and only smiled terrifyingly at little male dogs that tried to pick fights.

Then he disappeared again. On the second night I received a phone call – from a chef at the Magic Castle, a restaurant where famous conjurors and magicians from all over the world came to entertain diners. Booto had been a frequent visitor to the place, first discovering the kitchen, where he had endeared himself to the cooks for tasty titbits. From there, in his blunt and quietly pushing way, he had ingratiated himself into the main salon, where he was now being used as a 'straight man' in several tricks. A magician had discovered Booto's ability to bark loudly or with the merest whisper to order, and also his violent reaction to lighted cigarette butts. I watched one performance with fascination. The magician performed one trick, looked at Booto after the sparse applause, and said "What do you think of that?", whereupon Booto barked loudly. The magician turned to his audience: "Well, the dog likes it. What's wrong with *you* folks?" Then, with Booto grinning amiably on stage, he did another trick, asked Booto his opinion in a much quieter voice, and was rewarded with a scarcely audible "Whuff," whereupon the magician gave his audience one of those hurt Jack Benny looks, shrugged his shoulders, and sighed: "Yeah, I guess you're right. I never *could* get the hang of that trick anyway!"

Sometimes the magician tried to make Booto take uninteresting items in his mouth. At Booto's usual sneeze of refusal he hung a handkerchief from his table and said, "All right then, blow your nose!" If Booto didn't respond to a question – because he couldn't understand it – the magician said, "Well, he's thinking about it." Throughout his act he smoked cut-down cigarettes, casually tossing the lighted butts behind him. As Booto leaped upon them, furiously extinguishing them with his feet, the magician looked at the audience in feigned perplexity, as if unable to understand what was causing their roars of laughter. Booto was a great hit.

I had a hard task getting him back. The magician offered me first fifty, then a hundred and then a hundred and fifty dollars for him. There was no telling how high he might have bid had I not said I wouldn't sell Booto, even for a million. But I must confess I was a trifle jealous of Booto performing his tricks for someone else. There was no doubt about it: Hollywood was getting to Booto. He was beginning to understand and enjoy audience response, and he was becoming a real ham.

One day I went to the CBS studios to interview British star John Mills, who at 58 was rather gambling with his reputation after his distinguished career in British films by making a Hollywood TV series called *Dundee and the Culhane*. I expected the interview to be short, so instead of leaving Booto in the cottage I took him in the truck with me, making sure to park it in the shade, so we could have a jog in Griffith Park later. The interview, for Britain's *Daily Mail*, proved both sombre and even shorter than I'd anticipated, because the previous day CBS had decided to drop the show after only four weeks, and John Mills was returning to Britain, where at least he had new movie offers to consider. As I'd not had my usual invitation to lunch in the studio's best restaurant I went to the 'commoners' one, used by grips, carpenters, electricians and other workmen. I was standing in a short queue when I heard behind me an extremely familiar voice: "Hello, Mike, what are you doing over here?"

I turned, to find myself looking into the large brown eyes of Cary Grant! I was amazed, not only that he had recognised me after a single interview back in London over two years before, and that he remembered my name, but that such a megastar should be queuing up in the workmen's canteen.

We both had a light omelette lunch, during which Cary invited me to join him at his luxury suite at Universal Studios to try out a new champagne he was thinking of ordering. I said I'd have to walk my wild dog Booto first, and told him briefly how the dog came into my life. Cary said he would come with me. As I started tidying things up inside the truck, Cary took Booto's lead and said he would be happy to walk my dog, and what was more, Booto would be welcome to come with us to his suite instead of again being left in the truck. Once my chores were finished, I looked out – there was no sign of Cary or Booto. Cripes, was Cary Grant going to nick my dog? After about five minutes, to my great relief they reappeared round the side of a building.

Later, at his suite, Cary laughed with amused delight as I put Booto through some of his tricks. We both laughed even louder as I had taken in with me the new Peter Sellers record *The Best Of Sellers*, in which the comedy star's mimicry and impressions were excruciatingly funny. Cary laughed loudest of all in the scene where a common old dowager, played by Irene Handl, picks up an itinerant Frenchman (Sellers) on a park bench in a seaside resort and tries to inveigle him back to her hotel, saying it is a posh place "and they put croutons in the soup." Cary guffawed, slapped his knee, and repeated hysterically "They put croutons in the soup!"

Cary was so taken with the record he wondered how he could get a copy, to entertain some of his pals. I gave him mine on the spot, saying I could easily replace it through friends in Britain, although I never did get around to doing that. I won't forget that hilarious two hours with Cary Grant, as he had a fine sense of humour – and his champagne wasn't bad either. Alas, the planned jog with Booto round Griffith Park failed to happen that day.

The next major name to run his fingers through Booto's chestnut ruff was Omar Sharif, and to meet him we had to rattle out to a remote location in the deserts of Utah, where he was filming *Mackenna's Gold*.

Omar's most astonishing revelation was that since his divorce from Faten Hamama, whom he'd married in 1955 when she was Egypt's top movie star, he had become, filming apart, rather lonely, and he was now looking for the right kind of woman to marry. I felt quite startled that the man who played the passionate Sheikh Ali in *Lawrence Of Arabia* and the poetic *Dr Zhivago*, and had just co-starred with Barbra Streisand in *Funny Girl* – one of the ultimate male romantics of the current screen – should be having difficulty finding a new wife.

"For four years I have worked non-stop all over the world, living out of suitcases," he said. "Now I want to settle down, marry again, and have two more children – quickly." (He had a son, Tarek, from his marriage.) "And yet I don't seem to meet the kind of girl who would make me a good wife."

"Surely, it must be easy for a man in your position," I said. "One hears many stories of how women throw themselves at you."

He smiled. "No, that is the last kind of woman I would want. It is very difficult to find a woman who is prepared first of all to give *herself*. It is also very difficult for a good woman to live with an actor. There are such demands for publicity, appearances, to do things which enhance your career. There is little private life." At this point Omar, who was then 36 years old and a shade under six feet tall, began pacing up and down as if gathering his thoughts. I noticed Booto was looking at him intently – could see the dog had taken a liking to the man.

"The truth is, I find it difficult to live with a woman, for two people to be compatible all the time, to understand each other sufficiently to live in the same house 24 hours a day ... I want the kind of woman who will be just a woman, remain feminine and retain her intelligence. Most of all to be a woman to her man, as it were. It sounds simple enough, but women are becoming much more self-dependent, and most of them are not prepared to surrender all this."

He sat down suddenly, and seemed pleased when Booto walked over to him and thrust his shaggy head into his lap. Omar stroked Booto's fur as he continued talking.

"Of course there are some who are still capable of being what I want, but this kind of woman I don't get to meet ... I meet a lot of actresses, showgirls, a lot of society women. So these are the women I take out. But I don't particularly want to get involved, because I don't think – in general, of course – they make good wives.

"You see, I am trying to be extremely sensible in my life. I think marriage is something a man must enter in cold blood and not under the pressure of passion. One should enter marriage with real love, but that is something which takes time to develop – at least a year or more."

I was sure that stroking Booto's fur was making Omar more relaxed when talking on so personal a level. He raised one hand from Booto and poked me gently in the chest. "How do I go about finding, meeting girls from just normal families? How? Tell me!"

I said I didn't know, as I'd never been in his position. Would his future wife have to be attractive, I asked.

"I don't think I would love an unattractive woman," he replied. "But she need not be glamorous or very, very beautiful. She should be pretty, attractive, but most of all beautiful in her nature. Kind, feminine and able to accept me as the man, and to share my life but never try to run it."

He carried on in this vein, went into his childhood – "very privileged" – his early career, how he got his role in *Lawrence*: "Many people think I was just a native Bedouin boy who happened to wander up with his camel to where they were filming, and David Lean said 'Hey you boy ... do this ... say this ...'" He shook his head. "I had made twenty-four films in Egypt before *Lawrence*!"

The reason he spoke good English was because he went to the posh English school in Alexandria – Victoria College – which was run like a top English public school. He could also speak French, Arabic, Italian, Spanish and Greek fluently. For years he was also Egypt's top bridge player.

He told me how he won the musical role with Barbra Streisand although, as he told me, he had never sung before – "Not even in the shower!" He laughed. "William Wyler, the director, wanted someone who could wear beautiful clothes, had a lot of class, and could play a big-time operator. A man with all New York at his feet, but who falls in love with a girl just because she makes him laugh. Above all, Wyler wanted to stress the romantic side of the story.

"I was amazed when they called me in. But I decided not to do it if I couldn't sing my own songs. I walked into the audition thinking 'If I can't sing it's no shame, because I'm not *supposed* to be a singer.' All the top Columbia executives were there, plus the composer – and a piano. They said 'You've got to try.' So I did. I went right ahead and belted the songs out, and they all started clapping suddenly, and I had the part."

Just then there came a knock on the door. Omar was wanted for a conference on the next day's shooting with producer Carl Foreman and the director J. Lee Thompson. Sharif leaped from his chair, switched on a small record player, placed a disc on it, grabbed my shoulders and stood me in the centre of the room. "Stand here," he said. "This is a rough recording of one of my rehearsal songs with Barbra Streisand. Let me know what you think."

He left. The music started, and in that small motel room in the desert town of Page I became the first outsider to hear Sharif singing "You Are Woman, I Am Man!" from *Funny Girl*. His voice was strong, melodic, tuneful and full of authority. On his return Omar gave me two more hours of his time, and although I didn't realise it then, my interview with him was the most successful one on that whole Hollywood trip, for I sold it to leading magazines in five countries. As we parted, he gave a sad final pat to Booto, and said I was a lucky man to have such a companion.

"Maybe I would be better off getting a dog," Omar joked, as we shook hands and said au revoir.

—

Back in Hollywood Booto and I went to visit an actor friend of mine at the pool of his apartment building, but we stopped short at a sign that said 'Dogs Not Allowed.' "Don't take any notice of that," he said. "There's a noisy dog in there already, and if they chuck Booto out, they'll have to throw it out as well." The dog was a large, yapping poodle, the sort of hysterical canine, unsure of its place, often found in cities. It belonged to a permanent resident of the hotel, who seemed to feel her pet's 'high spirits' entitled it to make the lives of more transient guests a misery.

At first Booto ignored the poodle's noisy protests at the invasion of its domain by another dog. From under the shade of my deckchair he watched the idiotic creature prancing about, but when it came yelping towards us in its fourth mock attack, I said quietly "Get him, Boot!" Booto rushed out with a snarl, crouching low like a cat. The poodle took one closer look at the fearsome head and teeth, yelped with fear, and leaped back, falling with a great splash into the pool. To loud claps and appreciative laughter, Booto sneaked back behind my deckchair with what resembled a pleased grin.

One boiling hot day when I'd taken Booto in our truck to the beach at Malibu, where I often enjoyed a light lunch of oyster stew, a Los Angeles County beach buggy hurtled up. "Hey, dogs aren't allowed on the beach here buddy," said the official. "Didn't you see the signs?"

There had not been any signs where we hit the beach, but I said I was a Canadian on my way back to Canada, and had just stopped for a brief rest. He glared at my British Columbia number plates, and let me off with a rude caution. What sort of beach was that – no dogs allowed? It seemed a hint that our time in Hollywood was up.

6

With Booto in Mexico

After four months the appeal of the tinsel life had worn thin, and now the brief Californian winter was over, the heat was becoming stifling. In Hollywood one could buy everything one needed from just one supermarket – most unusual in the mid 1960s. All the healthy physical challenges of our life in the wilds had been removed. Life was easy – too easy – and Booto's waistline was spreading, along with mine. My own disenchantment with 'hotsmog city' was reflected in Booto, and as we walked along the neat, perfumed palm-fringed streets on our morning rambles he began to look very hangdog. Even the barking threats of the shaggy, bully Airedale across the road, who usually leaped out at passing canines and our moving truck, failed to bring more than a slight snarl to his lips. But at least my financial coffers were fairly full once more. I decided we had had enough of Hollywood, but before returning to our wilderness life in Canada we would tour Mexico in the truck.

I had a few valuable assignments there: to cover the 1968 Olympic preparations near Mexico City, to interview Dean Martin and Robert Mitchum, who were filming *Five Card Stud* on location near Durango, and also to report on the movie stars' hideaway, the seaside village of Puerto Vallarta.

It was just our luck, as we rumbled through the high mountains past Mazatlan, to first break a leaf spring, and then run into the first snow blizzards the area had suffered in fifteen years! We were trapped by the roadside for three days while I tried to teach Mexican bus, truck and car drivers that pouring water onto snow didn't melt it but turned it to ice.

As I was the only driver with a *pala* (shovel) I was tacitly appointed head scraper. After a few desultory scratches at the hard-caked snow, however, Booto gave it up as a bad job and showed he didn't want to leave the truck.

On the second night half a dozen thinly dressed members of a Mexican road gang came up with flashing smiles, empty beakers and plates, and started to climb aboard. I tried to explain about the broken spring, that I too had little food left – just a half-empty cereal packet, one can of milk, a tin of baked beans, and some dog biscuits. Booto began to growl, a low whining growl of warning as they paid no heed to my protests. In *their* country, completely outnumbered and without witnesses, there was no point in my getting belligerent.

Then, as one of the Mexicans reached out a hand for his dog biscuits, Booto leaped up with his paws on the back of the front bench seat, and with blood-curdling growls clashed his jaws together several times within inches of the man's face. The Mexicans instantly decided they weren't *that* hungry after all. and left in such a hurry that they momentarily got jammed in the door. I handed them half a dozen cigarettes through the window to placate them, and after this proof of at least *my* goodwill we were left alone for the rest of the night.

By the end of the third day most of the trucks, cars and buses had turned back, but I saw patches of blue sky appearing and felt a thaw was on the way, so decided Booto and I would stick it out until we could head on through to Durango. When I went to get my *pala* back, however, the Mexicans waved me away rudely. I returned with Booto on his lead. He hadn't spent time in the acting capital for nothing, and he could now, upon a word, produce a quite terrifying snarl, filled with white fangs.

Without a word the shovel was carefully placed before him like some sacrificial offering, and the ungrateful peons – I had done most of the shovelling over the three days – climbed hastily back into their vehicles.

When I began my work on the outdoor desert location of *Five Card Stud* I soon thought my busted leaf spring was just the start of some new troubles, as I dropped two large clangers on the first morning. The film's director was the tough, legendary Henry 'Hank' Hathaway, who was most certainly not a man to tangle with. Back in England I'd seen him boss even John Wayne about when filming *The Magnificent Showman*, and he even berated me for asking his new star Claudia Cardinale 'depressing questions'. I was therefore surprised and delighted when he said he remembered me, and even gave me permission to use my new camera, provided I didn't use it during actual shooting.

In the faint euphoria this aroused in me I heard Hank, who was setting up a scene, ask various technicians if all was well with them, and were they ready to go? When he added "And is it all right for you, Mike?" I replied, without thinking, "Yes, fine, thank you." There was a pregnant pause – then a great roar of laughter. Hank had been addressing the key grip, not me! Hank made an exaggerated bow towards me and said loudly "Oh, we are all *so* glad it is all right for the reporter from England!" I had seldom felt so small.

My second clanger came when Booto became a film actor. Hathaway had just set up a shoot-out scene for Dean Martin in a hot dusty street, and was lining up the next shot after extras had scattered just before a gun battle. "Quiet!" he shouted. "Okay – roll 'em!" In the eerie silence as the camera turned I saw to my horror that Booto was on the other side of the street. I had left him in the truck in the shade, with a high window opened because of the heat, but he must have climbed out. Just before the first pistol shot rang out Booto saw me, gave a little bark of recognition, rushed across the silent street like a hound from hell with tail between his legs, and started licking my hand.

"Who in hell owns that dog?" yelled Hathaway, whose crew had earlier spent an hour rounding up stray dogs, clucking chickens and crowing cockerels before the scene.

Fearing a public lambasting, and that I'd be thrown off the set, I shamefacedly stuttered: "I … I'm sorry. He's mine. I don't know how he got out of my truck." But to my great surprise Hathaway's face broke into its famous Churchillian grin. "Well, maybe you better pick up some pay," he beamed. "That dog is the best thing in the shot! He gave it more atmosphere!" Of course, I didn't want any pay, but in later conversation, when Hank personally introduced me to Dean Martin, I let it slip that my truck had suffered a busted rear leaf spring in the mountains en route. Hank said, "Well, we can fix that." And he organised the film's chief Mexican mechanic/blacksmith to make me a new leaf spring, beating the red hot metal to the right shape on his anvil and then fitting it – free of all cost to me. The best thing was that Hank left Booto's scene intact in the final film, and after all these years I still like occasionally to watch the video of my old canine compadre doing his bit part, as it is the only record I have of him on film.

After lunch Dean Martin came out of his trailer, looking slim and rakish in the black Stetson and the brown buckskin shirt and breeches he wore for his part, and began limbering up by shadow-boxing on his own. Hathaway called him away for a shot where he had to leap onto the shaft of two runaway horses. He did it, wiped the sweat from his brow, then called for his usual glass of slightly diluted whisky. (He was renowned in the movie business for liking the occasional tipple between filming shots.)

Well into my interview Dean told me he had made so many films back to back in recent years he really missed his huge family of *seven* children. "The only thing I hate about my life right now is wondering where my wife and kids are at this particular moment, and what they're doing. I really miss Jeanne and the kids when I'm miles away like this. And I'm not kidding. Already the three eldest have left home to live in their own apartments. When Deana goes soon there will only be three of them left." He shook his head, genuinely sad; then he grinned quickly. "I guess it must be my Italian blood – I love our big family. I suppose most people would consider three children at home to be enough, but to me it seems really quiet. I'm not looking forward to it really … one day they will all be gone. I know I shall feel lost without them."

Just then an assistant director came up to say that Dean was wanted for another tricky shot for the film. As I followed him back to where Hank Hathaway was waiting, by a wagon harnessed to two fretful horses, Dean said cryptically, "My stunt guy Bob ain't feeling so good today. Reckon I'll have to do this one myself." Dean bent down to say something to his stuntman, then lay down under the wagon, holding onto its rear axle with white knuckles. Hathaway, renowned for his toughness even with star actors, leaned down and said, "I don't want you to do this, Dean, even with the insurance. We can't replace you. Are you *sure* you really want to do this yourself?"

"Sure I'm going to do it," said Dean, from between the wheels. "You want it *real* don't you? Let's go."

"Okay. But you let go real soon – understand?" said Hathaway. He cued the cameras, head wrangler Tommy Sutton jerked the reins, and the horses bolted up the empty street. I took two photos as Martin's body bounced over the ground like a sack of rags, and after about twenty yards Hathaway wrung his hands in alarm, knowing if Dean dropped his head back he could break his neck.

"Let go! Let go, Dean!" he shouted.

Dean just hung on, his body raking up clouds of dust until he was almost out of sight. Then he let go, sat up with a grin, knowing there would be no need for a retake, twirled his gun expertly, and took an imaginary potshot at his director. When Dean came back to me I complimented him on his courage in doing such a dangerous stunt; so few highly paid stars would have tackled it personally. He gave a modest grin. "Well, not too bad for a 51-year-old granddad!"

In the revelation-filled interview that continued it was clear to me that Dean was far from his popular image as an affable, easy-going legendary free tippler and swinging womaniser, whose antics with 'The Clan' and in night clubs with Frank Sinatra had often made the headlines He was certainly easy-going, but he worked very hard, and had a great desire to keep things simple. When I asked him about the hard work, he replied: "Oh, you read about actors who say how hard they work. It makes me sick. Work like this is really only playing. I did this sort of 'work' as a kid – cowboys and indians. Now I'm highly paid for it!" He admitted he suffered from ulcers, and was no swinger in real life but fundamentally quite puritanical, being devoted to wife and family: most nights at home he was in bed by 10 pm. In fact, when he was next called away for another scene, after making sure no-one was looking, I reached for his half-empty glass and took a swig. It was not whisky, even diluted – it was cold, milkless *tea*!

There is no reason or room for my full interview here, but as I drove away from the location with Booto and my repaired truck to buy some food supplies, I saw some peasant children from the nearby village play-ing on some brand-new swings, a slide and a roundabout by their little wooden school. The brightly painted playground equipment contrasted strangely with the dust, sand and air of general poverty. I found out later that all the appliances were from a $2,000 gift to the children from Dean Martin. They seemed to fit in with the glimpse I'd just had of him – a glimpse perhaps of the real man.

That night I had a far tougher encounter, with the most enigmatic, iconoclastic, charismatic, witty, poetic, and possibly physically powerful movie star I ever met – Robert Mitchum. I had met him twice before, and although he always made it seem an accident that you and he hap-pened to be in a room at the same time, I got another cracking, even astonishing, interview with him. However, I will tell the full story of my meetings with Mitchum later in this book – after my fourth and final extraordinary encounter with him, just before I left my wilderness log cabin in Canada for the wilds of the Scottish Highlands.

With just this day's two star interviews in my notebooks our Mexican trip was already well into profit, as both would attract substantial fees from *Woman* and *Woman's Own* magazines in Britain, plus more from other top magazines worldwide. But I still had other commissions to fulfil: a report on travelling around Mexico, and another on the movie stars' 'hideaway' in the paradisical seaside resort of Puerto Vallarta for Canada's quality magazine *Chatelaine*. Also, a former colleague, the late Sir David English, who was then foreign editor of the *Daily Express*, wanted a precise report on how work was progressing on the new Azteca Stadium being built near Mexico City for the 1968 Olympics. We drove there first.

David was anxious to know the state, and possible advantages, of the newly invented 'Tartan' track. When we reached it a few Mexican workmen were at one end, laying the last outside stretches of the new rubberised track. All I knew was that it was composed of a three-quarter-inch carpet of hardened rubber solution mixed with rough rubber chips. At first I couldn't think of how to test the track, but I went to the side furthest away from the workmen and just jumped up and down on it. It certainly had a lot of 'bounce' in it, and I felt like the legendary

'Springheel Jack'. Then I hit on a far better idea: as a former Army athlete I could test it myself, by actually sprinting round it! I removed my jacket so that I was wearing only summer shirt, light slacks and gym shoes, got down into position, and then charged off on a 200 metre dash around the bend. I was swiftly conscious of fast, scuffling feet beside me. It was Booto, and I must confess that while he might have broken the human world sprint record, I came in a rather poor second. I was a bit winded, but I put this down to the altitude of the track, which was some 7,400 feet above sea level.

As I was recovering my breath a Canadian lady tourist came up and said she thought I'd run rather fast, and if I cared to do it again she would time me, and also take some photographs for me to keep, as I had to be the first human to run round the new Tartan track! This had not occurred to me, but now the idea had real appeal, and my jacket (and wallet) were over on the far side. Doing a second 200 metre bend would get me to them fast. Accordingly, a quarter hour later, I shut Booto in the truck and let the lady tourist do the "On your marks!" bit. This second bend was where the few Mexican workmen were still working, and as I was shooting halfway round I heard their irate yells of "Vamos!" and whatever was Mexican for "Get off the track!"

I felt I'd gone faster than the first time, so was more than gratified when the tourist said I had covered the distance in 24 seconds, which was almost as good as when I'd run for my Army battalion twenty years earlier. But I hadn't the slightest doubt that the Tartan track's resilient bounce had contributed greatly to this. It was a far cry from running round our old cinder tracks, when our feet sank in slightly with every step. In my report to David English I opined that the new track would knock about two seconds off the time of a top-class miler at normal altitude – which later proved to be just about correct. I was also right to predict that up to 400 metres world sprinting records would tumble on the new tracks, but here in Mexico the more rarefied air might give the long-distance men more trouble.

As I sought facts on how preparations were going, it was clear that in more ways than one Mexico had got more than it bargained for when offering to host the Nineteenth Olympiad. The bulldozers, working at a crashing pace to complete the Azteca stadium in time, had unearthed breathtaking relics of an earlier civilisation. The most exciting discovery was nine perfectly formed pyramids of the golden age of the Aztecs, 2,500 years ago.

Erwin Franz, supervising engineer, was excited. "It is astonishing that when the Games begin we will have the newest architecture and building in the world right next to what may prove to be the oldest archaeological site in the Americas."

As soon as the pyramids were discovered, a top anthropologist led the professional dig, working from daybreak to sundown cataloguing the finds. When preparing the site for the new Olympic village Erwin unearthed a large square court where the ancient Cuicuilco Indians kept their 'eternal fire' burning in a pit, and, in a supremely apt link with the past, that same pit was used to house the Olympic flame during the actual games.

He showed me a *pintadera*, a small stone cylinder that the Cuicuilcos covered with paint and rolled across their faces. Franz's pockets were stuffed with ancient earrings, arrowheads, and tiny stone idols found that very day. He handed me the *pintadera*, plus a face of a god broken off from the side of a Cuicuilco pot, and a tiny facsimile of a rain god's head in black stone, and said I could keep them as souvenirs, as they were not vital to their research. I have them to this day.

Erwin then showed me a small public burial pit he had found under the main pyramid. Two skeletons lay there, curled up in a foetal position. Booto sniffed at the bones suspiciously, but at some 2,500 years old they were of no interest to him.

Booto and I then toured the entire length of Mexico. For the next four weeks we were lost in the magical splendour of Mexico, which is perhaps the most 'foreign' of foreign countries. Dead mules and cattle, covered with black vultures, lay beside some of the smaller roads, yet in the towns the new Mexican architecture was the world's most modern. Twice at night, in this land of rich contrasts, we were motioned into the side of obscure mountain roads by fierce-looking, rifle-toting men. Fearing *bandidos*, I was relieved to find they were official guards, and the reason was nothing more sinister than a construction hold-up ahead – for Mexican road gangs often work at night by floodlight.

In our long drives I was soon aware of the vast grandeur of Mexico – eight times as large as the United Kingdom – and its wealth of holiday resorts, works of art, excursions to pre-Columbian remains, its mix of treasured baroque colonial art, ultra-modern architecture and extraordinary folklore. Its tropical climate is almost always pleasant, as most main towns are at high altitude. The land itself has exceptional geographic variety: the mountain peaks and great forests offer unique landscapes, the deserts and high plateaux have wild grandeur, and both its Pacific and Caribbean beaches are ideal for sunbathing, swimming, boating and underwater fishing. Mexico is not only the cradle of civilisation of the New World, but also the land that first felt the influence of that New World during the Spanish conquest led by Hernándo Cortes. A recent president, Gustavo Díaz Ordaz, explained that while tourism was vital to Mexico, it was not only for the money but also because the mix of cultures had a way of drawing peoples of the world together, leading to a better understanding of each other.

First, we drove to San Juan Teotihuacan to view the great pyramids of the Sun and the Moon. I looked at the towering pyramid of the Sun and felt somewhat daunted. But in the hope that it would 'keep my legs in' I set off up the steep steps, which were quite wide apart. With a series of little jumps Booto kept up with me, and we reached the top with hearts pounding. He found coming down a bit trickier, and had to achieve it with a series of doggy hops. After that, although it was not so high, we did not tackle the Moon!

We then headed south, as I wanted to see the ruins of the ancient city of Palenque, so after Veracruz we took the new Route 180, through the unremarkable oil towns of Minatitlan and Coatzacoalcos and on to the picturesque and more lovable, warm town of Villahermosa, which sits on the bank of a river and bustles with traffic, horse-drawn carriages, washerwomen, and a flourishing food market. From here we had to take to minor roads towards Chable, then turn right onto a rough jungle road still in the throes of being completed. There were occasional warning signs – *Derrumbe* (Falling rocks) and *Grava suelta* (Loose stones). We were spared these menaces, but the track was getting rougher, and before we reached the ruins I had to stop the truck and axe our way through a small tree that had fallen across it.

It was here that Booto saw his first iguana. Back in Canada he had loved chasing lizards, and when he saw the big iguana clattering its way metallically along a stony embankment he gave chase. But he got the shock of his life after leaping up the embankment and grabbing its tail in a swirl of sand, when the big lizard whipped round and fastened its jaws on his lip. He yelped, let go, and was left staring at eight inches of writhing tail as the iguana, by no means the humiliated loser, beat a hasty retreat.

As I stood on the edge of a clearing and looked at the temples – Temple of the Sun, Temple del Conde – I thought the Temple of Inscriptions might be worth a climb, but began to feel an oppressive atmosphere, a strange certainty that these ancient and magnificent relics would not appreciate my close presence or my boots on their surfaces, and certainly did not want to reveal any of their secrets to me. There was not another human in sight, and I felt very alone, but then I spied a white horse, calmly grazing below one of the temples. Where had it come from? Who owned it? Where was its stable?

We then left Palenque and the province of Chiapas, and set off for the wild deserts and scrubland of the mysterious Yucatan peninsula, where I hoped to visit the famous Mayan ruins of Chichén Itzá, and the sacred well of sacrifice, where the Maya-Toltecs sacrificed young girls and youths alive in drought periods to assuage Chac, the god of rain.

Going back down Route 180 again after Villahermosa I 'wasted' a day by taking the ferry to what I'd been told was the idyllic island town of Ciudad de Carmen, and I was not disappointed. I could happily live there – the streets filled with flowering bushes, an old-fashioned fishing fleet in the harbour, refreshing ocean breezes, a fabulous seafood meal that was probably still swimming when we were on the ferry, and heavenly beaches that seemed unexplored, and stretched for miles. There was a palm-lined street to the cemetery that was named El Ultimo Paseo (The Last Walk)! Booto and I swam in the cobalt seas for what seemed hours, and I had to book into a cheap motel for the night so that I could get enough fresh water to rinse the salt out of his fur, otherwise it would have been unpleasantly 'clogged up' for the rest of our journey.

Next day, heading on to Merida, we passed through the seaside town of Campeche, and endured seemingly interminable vistas of rough scrubland until we came to the spectacular Mayan ruins of Kabah and Uxmal, where we were charged only four pesos to park while we looked round the huge ancient edifice. Merida was a calm, tropical Spanish capital with horse-drawn carriages, and had an astonishing skyline of numerous windmills that lifted water from deep in the ground to supply the town's needs.

Yucatan has a basic limestone crust, which is dotted with caved-in pockets called *cenotes*. They fill with both percolated water and rain, and can make good wells or even swimming pools. Next day we drove the remaining seventy rather dreary miles to the famous ruins of Chichén Itzá, where I was surprised to find there were some thirty ancient structures one could examine. It was here we came to the object of our visit, and the grandfather of all wells. As I stood by the old altar on its rim and looked down over seventy feet of sheer wall into the murky depths of the sacred well of sacrifice, the whole place seemed bathed in a heavy, oppressive atmosphere, and I could understand the terror of its legend. Even Booto seemed to feel the presence of violent death, showing the whites of his eyes and walking about as if he were on ice. Well over 1,000 years ago, because they believed the rain god Chac inhabited this *cenote*, which is 180 feet across and nearly 60 feet deep, the ancient Mayans threw offerings of precious objects and even human beings, mostly young, into its waters. Sometimes the victims' hearts were torn out and offered first. When the Mayans abandoned Chichén Itzá and were replaced by the more militaristic Toltecs, the sacrifices were continued. Scientific examination of the remains from the Maya-Toltec period (AD 925–1200) has shown that these three centuries were probably the peak for human sacrifice, as the Toltec priests also supported the practice.

In the spirit of the culture you had to give Chac your most precious possession, and if that happened to be a daughter or son, you gave them up willingly. Even the child was supposed to die happily, because it was in a glorious cause – the child was going to plead with Chac about the people's needs. Most of the skulls found in the well are of children between eighteen months and twelve years old.

As I stared down into the *cenote*, reflecting on its bloody past, I suddenly felt strangely dizzy, and had to suppress a feeling of vertigo – a frightening desire to throw myself down. Calling Booto away, I abruptly left the place. My camera had run out of film, but although I could easily buy more in such a touristy place, I had no wish to go back and take pictures. I drove many miles of our return journey that afternoon, in order to put as much distance as possible between us and that awful place before we camped for the night.

Next morning I decided to suffer the frights and risks of driving in congested Mexico City again, as I wanted to visit the glorious new Museo Nacional de Antropología, which housed the greatest collection of pre-Columbian art in the world. It, and the startlingly modern building itself, are worth a trip to Mexico on their own. I was lucky enough to be given written permission to photograph some of the most spectacular and priceless exhibits. Unfortunately, unable to read Mexican, I hadn't a clue what most of them were, and would have to seek scholarly advice later!

Now I had only one job left – that visit to the new movie stars' hideaway on the sea at Puerto Vallarta for the Canadian magazine, *Chatelaine*. That meant more hard driving, and when we were 1,500 miles further north we turned west above Guadalajara, north to Tepic, then south to Compostela, where the remaining hundred or more miles to Puerto Vallarta were over rough, rutted dirt track through jungle. Once I had to stop and use my crowbar to lever away a great chunk of sandstone rock that blocked our way. It was while I was doing this that Booto got his next great shock of our trip. He had hopped out to obey a call of nature when he suddenly put his nose to the ground, smelled 'cat', and disappeared into the trackside foliage.

Fifty yards away, as I gave chase, I saw him stop, leap backwards, make a loud bark, then rush after a long-tailed spotted animal. It was an ocelot. As he pursued it up a sloping tree trunk, it whirled round, spat loudly, and narrowly missed Booto's nose with a slashing swipe of its claws. Booto, greatly chagrined by the enormous size of this 'cat', and by nearly losing his nose, ran back to me with ears flattened and the oddest look of humiliation on his face.

In Puerto Vallarta Booto and I had a great time, and leading local luminaries, bar and cafe owners seemed quite anxious to extol the delights of what had become the movie stars' hideaway. I found out that John Wayne sailed his yacht here down from the Baja California to fish, and the parties he threw on the Los Muertos beach were very popular.

"He was the life and soul, talked to everyone. For such a big-name star he seems a very humble, nice guy," Pura Bilbao who ran the celebrities' bar at the Oceano Hotel, told me. Rock Hudson, Lana Turner and Ralph Bellamy were regular visitors. Marlon Brando was building a house on the outskirts, and Ava Gardner water-skied most mornings to the location set at Mismaloya when filming *Night Of The Iguana* with Richard Burton and Elizabeth Taylor.

Liz Rubey, a leading socialite, said, "No-one here cares if you are a movie star or not. In fact you have to have something extra to be popular. Stars come to relax – to get away from high-pressure socialising. In Hollywood, where so many are forced to show all, they are in danger of becoming all show! In Puerto Vallarta they can escape – to fish, drink, swim, chat in the bars and visit each other like everyone else. And they aren't harassed by fans. Very few are ever asked for autographs. Even Elizabeth Taylor could sit outside Pura Bilbao's bar and not be bothered."

In fact it was Liz Taylor and Richard Burton who first put what had been a sleepy fishing village on the map. They were lovers here in 1964 before their marriage in Montreal, when John Huston was directing them (along with Ava Gardner, Deborah Kerr and Sue Lyon) in *Night Of The Iguana*. At the time the eyes of the world's media were glued to the pair, and they so loved the place they each bought a house on Guerrero Street – which was later nicknamed 'Gringo Gulch' from the many Americans who subsequently rushed and bought homes there.

Roberto Wong, who ran the Burton's favourite bar at the Rio Hotel, told me how to find the houses, and gave me an amusing little story about them. "You go to the end of the little street and you will come to the Casa Kimberley on the left. That is Miss Taylor's. Mr Burton's is across the other side of the street. People here smile when they go past," he added, "and you will see why. They were not yet married but they wanted to be together. So they had a little 'love bridge' built over the street to connect their homes! I think they did not live in the same house because they did not want to offend the local people. Mexicans, you know, are very puritan."

I went up the Saraguza to the cobblestone hills above the port, turned right, then left into Gringo Gulch, and there they were: Miss Taylor's house, an imposing four-storey villa with two white patios that leaned over the street, and from them the love bridge, of white stone with Venetian-type balustrades, stretching across into the one top room of Burton's residence, which was a long, rambling structure of brick and grey stone. I soon learnt that between their visits, millionaires or not, Burton and Taylor rented out their houses.

As I took photos, a woman tenant rushed to the balcony of Miss Taylor's house. "Don't worry," she called sarcastically, "Richard and Liz will be with you in a moment!" She was clearly pretty tired of inquisitive tourists.

It took me a week to complete my report on Puerto Vallarta, and every night we camped out under palm and coconut trees on a lonely paradisical sandy beach outside the port. I even found the hotel and other buildings that had been erected at a cost of many thousands of dollars for *Night Of The Iguana* amid the luscious, dark green tropical foliage outside the sleepy little village of Mismaloya. All were now empty, deserted and shuttered. An eerie silence prevailed amid the beauty, broken only by the scuttlings of iguanas, two feet long, across the red tiled roofs.

I found out in the village that the peasants would not move into the buildings because they had no *cocinas* (kitchens), and were too draughty. Also, the peasants were suspicious of foreign-made buildings and pre-ferred their thatched huts.

I had the sudden idea to try and acquire the buildings myself, if I could borrow enough money. This notion vanished when I found out that, at that time, no foreigner could actually own land within five ki-lometres of the beach in Mexico. All this new glimpse of paradise had in fact achieved was to increase my wish to tie up my last business in Hollywood and hasten back to Canada and find paradise again on the wild, abundant coast that Booto and I loved.

On our last day in Hollywood I accepted an invitation to that year's Oscar Awards. My friend from London and I, all togged up in hired evening suits, and with Booto grinning widely between us, turned up in my ugly great milk truck amid the polished Lincolns, Cadillacs and Buicks. The mouths of the traffic police fell open in surprise, and at first they frantically waved us to get out of the way. Then one of the police ushers saw the big orange Oscar Awards permit on the windscreen, gave me a look of apparent recognition, and said, "Aha, Warren! Come this way!" and showed us where to park further along. As the truck drew up before the vast auditorium, where TV interviewers were greeting the stars as they alighted from their luxury cars, a big roar went up from the crowd. As some youngsters demanded autographs, we protested in vain that we were not stars – or even actors.

"It must be the dog then," said one baffled lad. "Who is it – Lassie?"

During his wise-cracking introductory repartee, master of ceremonies Bob Hope got a big laugh when he said, "Did you see that big grey truck? That was Warren Beatty – he brought the truck to carry away all his Oscars!" (For *Bonnie And Clyde*.)

Enormously flattering though it was to be mistaken for Warren Beatty, it all seemed a fitting goodbye to Tinsel Town.

Next day, as I packed the final items into the truck for the long haul back to Canada, Booto sat disconsolately on the tailboard. Perhaps he thought he was going to be left behind – as he nearly had been in Canada. As I pushed the last books into the bookcase, the large, bullying, shaggy Airedale ran across the road and began the barking barrage it often used to express its dislike of country bumpkin Booto's presence in its road. I watched Booto lying there, his toes curled over the rear of the truck's floor, and could see all the long-suppressed annoyance rising within him.

Before I could stop him, he leaped off the truck, dived under the larger dog and, ignoring its teeth in his neck ruff, flipped it three feet into the air. As it landed on its side, Booto went in again like a flash, pinning it on its back. The dog still showed fight, so Booto slashed it across the ear and stomach, and it ran back to its home, bleeding, and yelping with pain and fear. Booto returned to the truck with an almost apologetic look that said "Sorry, but he had it coming."

It was one of the few times I'd seen his wolf blood come to the fore, but we made a strategic and hurried exit from Hollywood. I kept my foot on the gas, and although the old truck could not exceed 55 miles an hour, and I had only half an hour's rest, we covered the 1,382 miles to Vancouver in 38 hours. Four hours later, after a ferry trip, we were back at my little wooden cabin overlooking the Pacific ocean. I was alarmed at first when I saw its door was slightly ajar. Someone must have picked the lock. But nothing had been stolen, and on my spruce little driftwood desk was an unsigned note that said "Thanks for the good night's rest." And beside it was a bottle of my favourite local Calona red wine.

I spent the rest of that year finishing my novel, improving my cabin and, on fine days, just sinking myself into the wonderful way of life in the wilds. It seemed ironic that I was now living with great joy on about five dollars a week, yet I was doing everything – sunbathing, swimming, fishing, rowing, trekking the wild places – that everyone I had left behind was slaving and saving for during their short holidays each year. Yet for me it had become just part of a natural way of life, living close to the animal state – not just a brief, frenzied escape, when years of city life have so blunted the senses that one barely understands the manifold subtleties of the wilderness. I still had a lot to learn, but what a hard but marvellous open-air university!

Of course, money eventually became a problem, but that winter I managed to line up some top commissions from leading magazines in several countries to try and get in-depth stories on stars such as Robert Mitchum, Doris Day and Steve McQueen. If I pulled them all off I should have enough money to last another year in the Canadian wilds. This time I did not take Booto with me, not because I didn't want to, but because during the long periods when I was writing my book he got bored, and had been spending a lot of his time a few miles up the forest road with Fred Jackson and his wife. He shared his favours between us, and the Jacksons were more than pleased to look after him while I was away.

Most of the magazines, and even the *Daily Mail* in Britain, wanted Robert Mitchum, so I decided to tackle him first. I had met the old maverick several times over the years and considered him to be the most baffling, complicated and charismatic star I'd ever met, so I shall now tell the full story of my meetings and experiences with him.

7

The Maverick

Robert Mitchum was probably the only man in the world with a legitimate income of over a million dollars a year who had served three terms in jail: seven days on a chain gang in Georgie for vagrancy in 1933 when he was fifteen years old; two days after a family squabble in 1945; and fifty days on a narcotics charge in 1949, where the word 'marijuana' seemed the very embodiment of evil. A hippy thirty years before the word was invented, his youthful life was as indigenously early American as Huckleberry Finn. At fourteen, after a poverty-stricken and rebellious childhood, he ran away from home and became a rod-riding hobo on the trains, crossing America nine times. For the next ten years before he got into movies in 1942, by mastering a vicious horse that threw him three times, he worked as a deckhand on a salvage boat, a mine worker, tree planter, dish washer, longshoreman, truck loader, professional boxer, song writer and sheet metal worker.

Through his movie career he was the last of the original Hollywood rebels, and one who never became pretentious. No-one put Mitchum down more than Mitchum himself. I once asked him how he had lasted so long (he made over 100 films in his life). "I've survived because I work cheap, don't bang into the furniture, and know my lines," he replied.

Mitchum was recognised by the Hollywood cognoscenti, the top directors and producers, as one of the finest screen actors alive, and as one of the few stars left whose name along could pull audiences into the cinema. Could he analyse his appeal, I once asked him.

View from my cliff-top log cabin in Canada. A beachcomber removes free logs drifted from the log booms. Luckily, I'd already taken enough for my cabin.

For months I lived largely off the sea, so prolific in British Columbia in the mid 1960s I could in one hour catch enough fish for a week.

My pal Geordie Tocher with the small canoe outrigger he made to go out with his huge newly carved Haida war canoe, in which he later sailed to Hawaii.

Felling a large dead fir tree with chainsaw and axe.

Me with Booto taking a driving break in the first mountains of Mexico.

We lived in my old milk truck/camper.

Our old milk truck/camper stuck in the mountains on the way to Durango in first snow blizzards for many years. We were stuck for four days.

I visited Dean Martin on the outdoor set of Five Card Stud *near Durango, Mexico, and photographed him doing dangerous stunts.*

Dean Martin performing his own stunts on the outdoor set of Five Card Stud *near Durango, Mexico.*

With his stuntman ill, Dean did this one himself – being dragged at high speed over rough ground for over a hundred yards. Tough director Hank Hathaway was afraid he would break his neck.

Testing the newly laid 'Tartan' track of the 1968 Olympics, for the Daily Express. *I was the first human to run round it. The Mexican workmen were not pleased!*

A couple of the many ancient temples and palaces in the jungle at Palenque, Mexico.

The eerie, empty village movie set costing thousands of dollars for Night of the Iguana. *It could have made a wonderful small resort but I could not legally own it.*

When doing a magazine report on the movie stars' 'hideaway' at Puerto Vallarta, Mexico, Booto and I camped on an idyllic nearby beach. I cracked free coconuts!

Fire Down Below (1957)

Taciturn in Ryan's Daughter with Sarah Miles (1970)

El Dorado (1966)

Farewell, My Lovely (1975)

Smitten by Marilyn Monroe in River of No Return (1954)

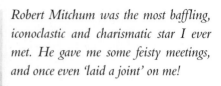
Robert Mitchum was the most baffling, iconoclastic and charismatic star I ever met. He gave me some feisty meetings, and once even 'laid a joint' on me!

Robert Mitchum with wife Dorothy, who was his boyhood sweetheart and to whom he remained married all his life.

Doris's choice: cycles not Cadillacs

Doris Day with her manager–husband Marty Melcher, who master-minded the business side of her career.

Doris Day cycling to shops in Beverley Hills. She gave me a great interview in her home, and even offered me a film test.

Steve McQueen with wife Neile.

Steve McQueen relaxing after our motorbike rides.

Me interviewing John Wayne. The world's most popular star gave me more of his time than any other star, and even let me spend two days with his wife, for the Woman magazine's angle.

Omar Sharif during his actual rehearsals for Funny Girl co-starring Barbra Streisand.

My last night at my log cabin in Canada, sitting on edge of cliff below cabin.

Boating downriver with North America's leading Indian guide, Clayton Mack, in dangerous grizzly bear country. He liked to show off his mastery of the jet-engined boat.

Clayton Mack (on the left) with one of his wealthy American hunters. He took me on exciting and successful treks among the big bears.

We eventually reached the marshy tidal flats where grizzlies came to graze at dawn and dusk.

Young cougar taking refuge up a tree from human and dog.

Mother grizzly with two well-grown cubs rearing onto hind haunches to look out for danger.

Large black bear at the city dump outside the Indian reserve at Bella Coola. These bears can lose their fear of man and are therefore dangerous.

After the grizzly treks with Clayton Mack I went to say a final goodbye to wild dog Booto who I had not seen for nearly five years. I could hardly believe the sad old dog who greeted me was him.

For me, it was indeed a tearful farewell.

"Sure, I bring a ray of hope to the great unwashed. I look like I've changed a million tyres. Hell, I *have* changed a million tyres! The typical Mitchum fan is full of warts and dandruff. He sees me up there on the screen, a ten-foot masturbation image, and he thinks 'Gee, if that big bum can make it, I can be President of the United States.' I've lasted because I trade on public amazement. People pay to see my films so that they can marvel and say 'Is that old son of a bitch still there?'"

His wit was épée sharp. When he went back to Savannah, Georgia, the scene of his chain gang stint, someone asked him, "How do you like it *now* in Savannah?" Mitchum replied, "Man, I like it where I can git it!" When a middle-aged woman fan stopped him once and said she had seen and loved all his films, he smiled at her kindly, and drawled "Lady, save your money."

He refused to admit that he took his film career seriously. "Look," he told me once, "I came into being during the era of the ugly leading man, and I always made the same movie. They just kept moving new leading ladies in front of me. I woke up once and there was Marilyn Monroe (*River of No Return*). They said 'Look, we got all this rubbish to unload and we'll pay you to help us unload it.' Well, it sure beats working! People started talking about Mitchum-type roles, but I never knew what they meant. Paint my eyes on my eyelids, man, and I'll sleepwalk through it. The least work for the most reward."

Despite his flamboyant, apparently careless image, Mitchum had a reputation for professional reliability. He was never known to be late on a film set, and he not only knew his own dialogue cold, but often everyone else's words too. He had been known to drink all night and still not fluff a line next day. Behind the wit and outward cynicism I found lurking an acutely sensitive and artistic nature. He could play the saxophone well, and once composed an oratorio that was performed at the Hollywood Bowl. He wrote songs, and one, 'The Ballad of Thunder Road', recorded in his own soft baritone in 1958, hit the top and stayed in the top 100 for four years. He wrote poetry, too, which appeared in several esoteric literary magazines. One of my favourites was the one he wrote to his mother at fifteen when he was hoboing around America:

Trouble lies in sullen pools along the road I've taken.
Sightless windows stare the empty street.
No love beckons me save that which I've forsaken.
The anguish of my solitude is sweet.

His sensitivity is shown in this little poem he wrote about his seven-year-old daughter Trina:

How about this child!
With the fresh smell of April
And tears cheering the heartbroken smile of her hope
And moist-handed
Praying in song so rich
That listeners die
Upon its wish.

I met Bob Mitchum four times over the years, and on three of those occasions I asked him why, after such an extraordinarily adventurous life, he hadn't written his life story. The first time he said, "What for? The Los Angeles police have it all on file." The second time he replied, "No way, I'd have to leave town. I've had trouble enough." And the third time he told me, "I can't spell! Anyway, I think it would have little value."

I always approached any interview with him with a kind of nervous excitement, not only because he made it seem like an accident that you and he were in the same place together, but because he often liked to shock – to test the interviewer's credentials.

I'll never forget our first meeting. I can't remember the actual film he was working on, but it was at Elstree in the late 1950s, when I'd just landed a prestigious show business column. We were going through some of his earliest memories, and at one point I suggested he'd had a most unusual boyhood.

"It sure was," he agreed. "At one time my mother, sister and brother were living on a farm while our stepdad had to work in the town. I was sometimes sent to stay with an aunt. *She* was unusual 'cos she was a hooker, and she had a speciality. She had one normal eye and one glass eye. For a few dollars more she would take out her glass eye – and blink 'em off!" I was so shocked, I dropped my notebook, which was precisely the reaction Mitchum had intended.

I managed to recover enough to tease out of him some amusing anecdotes about his tumultuous early life, and a few caustic comments about the film business and some of the top stars in it – enough for a lively column, anyway.

The second time I met him was some ten years later, when he was on location in Ireland for the film *Ryan's Daughter*. It had been reported that, because of the protracted schedule, he'd got so bored he'd even stopped drinking. Once again he put me on the spot. Although I'd arranged the interview through the publicity department, when I obeyed Mitchum's peremptory shout "Come in!" I entered his dressing room and found him lying prone on his back on a huge sofa – with his hat over his face.

I asked him a couple of neutral questions, but couldn't hear his mumbled answers because of the hat. I took a chance: "Well," I said loudly, "you're the only movie star I ever met who really *did* talk through his hat!" There was a minor explosion – "Goddam!" – and Mitchum jackknifed up to a sitting position, clasped his hands together with his elbows resting on his knees, looked me straight in the eyes, and said, "Okay, what do you wanna know?"

Perhaps the most amazing fact about him was that, despite his philandering image, he was now the only major star who was still married to his childhood sweetheart, the girl he wed *before* he became an actor. He met dark-haired Dorothy Spence in Delaware when he was sixteen and still had the chain gang shackle marks showing on his ankles. "In only a couple of days it didn't matter what I said or what she said, we both *knew* this was it," Robert told me. He went back to his hobo life on the road, but between his odd jobs he kept going back to tell Dorothy to wait until he had a decent stake. After working as a ghost writer to top astrologer Carroll Righter, Robert had saved up $2,400, and at age 23 he went back to claim Dorothy as his wife.

He laughed at a memory: "I left Florida where it was ninety-five degrees in the shade, got off the Greyhound bus wearing a thin ice-cream suit and a Panama hat, and fell onto my nose into four feet of snow. I told Dorothy my sad story, and she said 'I don't think you're fit to be let loose any more. I'd suggest we get married' – which is what *I* had been planning all along!"

Over the years, with his ultra-busy filming schedule, the couple had a few quarrels, and twice they were separated for short periods, but there was never any talk of divorce. Their three children – Jim and Chris, both actors, and daughter Trina – were all well-balanced youngsters.

"It sure has been difficult for Dorothy at times" he admitted to me. "I'd say adaptability has been her greatest quality." Then he smiled. "Look, our marriage has lasted because we adopted the course of least resistance. Dorothy used to throw me out of the house, along with a few of my wild pals. I mean – *regularly*! Finally I said, 'Look honey, I can't pack any more. If anybody's going to go, *you're* going to have to go, because I'm not going any place.' So that was the end of that. She's never mentioned it since."

Robert told me he had always been very fond of his wife, and in many ways her patient and stable nature had helped to civilise him and stop him from 'going native'.

As I was interviewing him, this time for a leading women's magazine, this talk about his marriage enabled me to prise out his views on modern women, feminism, trends between the sexes and so forth, and he came up with some really fascinating and deep-thinking material, so my trip to Ireland proved, for me, a huge success.

It was way out in the broiling desert near Durango, Mexico, when he was filming *Five Card Stud* with Dean Martin, that I met Robert for the third time. If I was surprised that he did not try to put me on the spot again, I was even more so when our conversation took a serious note, and he put on a dazzling display of verbal pyrotechnics and proved he could discuss almost any subject with keen insight. He often quoted his favourite lines from classical books to illustrate points, using what was clearly a prodigious memory. (Bear in mind here that our meeting took place in late 1968.)

I asked him if he agreed that what we called 'brainwashing' in communist China and the East was matched only by increased thought-conditioning in the West, caused partly by trivial TV and the onslaught of advertising, where the trivialisation of fine human emotions helped make people believe that material success – the use of this face cream, that hair tonic, this car, that set of books, and so on – would make them happier and better people.

"Oh, I know there is thought-conditioning on TV, but it's trivia. Its got to be all hokey, hasn't it? The faster they kid the people, the faster the public catch on, and people like the hippies, for instance, are way, way ahead of many of the people who control the TV medium. So are the Negroes, and they are hungry for social change and real equality, if not more.

"I agree it's hard for young people to be truly individual today: they are pressured from all sides. But the trivia on TV separates the men from the boys. A large portion of the people accept and believe the trivia, and you have a nation of granny gooses. But you will have that anyway – just as you'll get uncreative spoilers and throwbacks in any race or nation.

"The United States is the most materially developed nation in the world. And it has projected itself in time. There is a group of people in their twenties today to whom any significant breakthrough is meaningless, just like the next chapter in a TV show. No more than that."

I knew it was rare to hear Robert Mitchum open up like this, but it gave me a glimpse at least of the deep-thinking man behind his two-fisted, movie star image.

"Not long ago, man first broke the sound barrier," he went on, "a great breakthrough. Then the nuclear fission barrier. Then the time barrier, which everyone said could not be broken. But, hell, we have cracked that too. Whatever happened to those funny little things like radio which used to fill us with wonder? It's *all* communications today, and it has resulted in a general symposium of thinking, hasn't it?

"You can bang information and messages and ideas and news off the moon or a satellite today, and everyone knows what is happening at the same time. They all see it, and hear the same words about it, at the same time. It's bound at first to lead to a similar thinking generally. But it doesn't mean it will *stay* that way. At least we have an advanced peasantry, don't we?

"What we have to keep pressing for in the individual is *awareness* of what is going on. For education and communication – communication of real values. It's the only hope. Ignorance leads to prejudice on all levels, doesn't it? So all the kids who are wipeouts – I don't call them cop-outs – the wipeouts really become aware of what it's really all about. Rebellion for its own sake is meaningless. Look at many of these kids! Their faces show *nothing*. If only these kids striking in the universities today knew what they were really talking about! If only they had some real *experience* of life, instead of getting bedded down in their half-baked, quasi-wipeout philosophies!"

He gave a slight sigh and brief shake of his head, then went on: "Perhaps it is a minority of youth that behaves this way though, an over-publicised minority too, which gives them more strength. But it is not only youth who agitate publicly without any true knowledge of life. There are others who have purpose, and want to achieve their goals with violence. One hope is that they always seem to lose individuality and order. Eventually I find they become very conservative. Yes, almost all of them, even the violent groups. When they do learn they often become *very* conservative. What they are doing much of the time is jerking, jerking at our jackets and saying 'Look, look at me!' And that's really all. Often the knowledge behind their public agitation is puerile and naïve."

He stopped talking suddenly. I felt he thought he'd said too much – that it was not really his business to talk this way.

"And yet," he added more quietly, "as soon as you get a group of these young people together – and there is someone with enough insight who can tell them why they are there – they will listen." (Mitchum had fulfilled requests to give several seminars at universities, although he did not actually lecture.) "We need good teachers – and good writers. I always like writing, but I guess I'm too lazy, and for me it's too revealing. Besides, it's a little too late … I think sometimes I ought to go back and try to do at least one thing well. But again, indolence would probably cause me to hesitate about finding a place to start."

Bob Mitchum's 'indolence' was, I'm convinced, caused by an innate shyness. He several times told me he was a 'natural hermit', and that he had really been in 'a constant motion of escape' for most of his life, and I believed him.

I had to leave him then, as he had to go over his script for the following day. He had also told me that acting was the least important thing in his life, because it interfered too much with his social – and intellectual – life. But if people were prepared to pay him to do it, at least he tried to do a professional job.

My fourth meeting with Robert Mitchum came about in unusual circumstances. It was when I had been living in the wilds of western Canada for two years, and had decided to take a winter drive to Hollywood in my old milk truck and bag a few star interviews so I could pay my way for another year in the Canadian wilderness. I had commissions from leading magazines in several countries to try and get in-depth articles and all of them most wanted Mitchum.

On arriving in Hollywood I booked into the cheap but excellent Montecito Hotel (it also had a fine pool) and went straight to the library of the Motion Picture Academy, where librarian Bonnie Rothbart piled thick packets of cuttings about Mitchum onto my desk. As I leafed through them I realised that, if I could get one more good chat with him, with the material I already had I could put together a pretty good biography of the star, never mind the mini-series that women's magazines wanted.

The trouble was, he was not currently making a film, so I could not go through the usual studio publicity route. Instead, I had to work through his ultra-efficient manager-secretary Reva Frederick, who, with a small staff, ran all his business interests from the office of his own film company Talbot Productions on Sunset Boulevard. Reva, originally a friend of Mitchum's half-sister Carol, started out doing part-time secretarial chores but when his career took off in the late 1940s and he was snowed under with paper work she went to work for him full time.

It was soon obvious from talking to Hollywood contacts that anyone who wanted to meet, proposition, or even just telephone him had to first go through Reva Frederick. And so, trying to muster up what little charm I might have left, and wearing the only suit I *did* have left, I was soon in her office.

Reva, who was good-looking enough to have been in films herself, was quite charming and said yes, she probably *could* get me some copies of photos from the Mitchum family albums for my women's magazine pieces. But when I asked if she could possibly prevail upon Mitchum to meet me again, she said she would try, but it would be "very tricky as he's at home in private time". If I rang her the following afternoon she would let me know when to pick up the photos. When I did so, I was naturally anxious to know whether her boss had agreed to meet me. Reva said she *had* asked Mitchum, but he had given a non-committal answer. However, I could pick up half a dozen photos from her tomorrow at midday.

I reached the office dead on time, and was delighted, when looking through the photos, to find one of Robert as a schoolboy, and one on the beach with his brother John as teenagers – both slim, athletic, with wide shoulders. There were others of the whole family round their dinner table and on a camping holiday, and a happy one of Robert relaxing at home with wife Dorothy, with both their faces wreathed in smiles. And all the photos were exclusive to me.

Suddenly the door burst open, and a big man bounced in, wearing tight pants, colourful tailored silk shirt, and stylish Le Mans sunglasses. He had a mad, trendy hairstyle, and an expensive camera slung over his back, and at first I thought he was some big, cocky paparazzi photographer trying to bulldoze his way into the Mitchum ménage. What a nerve!

But no. As he removed the sunglasses I realised it was the original hobo-ing hippie himself – Robert Mitchum, now 54 but looking almost as young as he did in 1948 when he got jailed for fifty days for smoking cannabis. I could hardly believe it; in a recent film, *El Dorado*, when he co-starred with John Wayne, he'd looked jowly, paunchy, grey-bearded, but now he looked impossibly fit for a man his age, trimmed down to around 190 pounds, the huge shoulders still taut and powerful. How had he achieved this new lean look?

"Drink," he growled. "Drink is what does it. Alcohol is like embalming fluid. You can't get old if you're pickled!"

He took a deep gulp of the ice-cold beer Reva hastily handed him. "What's with the camera?" I asked. "I'm a peeping Tom," he replied. "Now I can afford to be one in style!"

A long and memorable interview followed, and he filled in for me a few crucial gaps in his life story. I told him I had been surprised during my research at the library to find that in early 1951 the Los Angeles court had quietly reviewed his marijuana conviction and dismissed the guilty verdict. While millions had heard of his jail term, hardly anyone had heard of his exoneration. "Well, that's the press for you," he said wryly. "I didn't want to publicise it myself – not important." And that's all he would say.

It was after he had treated me to a long discourse on the history of marijuana, its social effects and the question of legalisation, that I asked him directly: "I take it you're not still on pot?"

He gave me a look, reached down into a pocket suddenly, and flipped me a hand-rolled cigarette. "Oh yeah? Try that."

To my great surprise Mitchum had, just like that, 'laid a joint' on me.

"Is this the real stuff?" I asked him.

"How would *you* know?"

My mind shot back to the time I'd tried a joint with the Mexican photographers. I took a few puffs and made the customary deep inhalations. "It's the real stuff," I said. "The full Acapulco gold!"

Mitchum raised his eyebrows and gave Reva a wry, amused nod. I asked him if he was going to smoke one. He held up the mug of ice-cold beer Reva had given him. "Beer doesn't need a mix," he said. He didn't smoke.

The interview was over. I thanked him and Reva and made my exit, meaning to go on to the library to finish my research, but as I walked along Sunset Boulevard I suddenly felt most strange. I stopped – on the corner of Sunset and Vine, wracked by indecision. Should I go on to the library? Or should I go back to my hotel and retrieve all my notes on Mitchum, which I had stuffed below the mattress on my bed? I had let slip a hint that I was considering writing a book. What if he and Reva didn't like the idea? Would they send someone to grab my notes? Would they ask the library not to cooperate with me? I just couldn't make up my mind. I stood there for a good five minutes, unable to decide what to do, before common sense forced me to proceed to the library – where all was well. The marijuana had relaxed my mind so much that for a good while I'd been unable to make a decision. It was really scary. And the fact that I have never smoked pot since, or even held a joint, is due entirely to Robert Mitchum.

~

When Robert Mitchum died in his sleep one month short of his 80th birthday in 1997 it seemed entirely fitting he was at home with his wife Dorothy.

8

America's Sweetheart

I could hardly believe I was sitting in Doris Day's Hollywood home, or that 'America's Sweetheart' was looking into my eyes and saying what she was saying … I had enjoyed a fabulous long interview about her life and career as singer, dancer and actress that had made her the world's favourite woman star, when suddenly she asked me: "Mike, have you ever done any acting?"

I felt flummoxed at first, then I recalled my youthful attempt to be an entertainer like Al Jolson. She had a good laugh when I told her how that ambition had ended in the single night of my disastrous debut on stage – when the theatre audience had greeted my performance with total silence, and not a single hand clap! But why did she ask if I'd done any acting?

"Well, you're a good-looking guy, and I think we ought to give you a film test. You look a lot like Rock Hudson, but you're not so *big*. If you were any good I wouldn't have to keep standing on orange boxes in the clinches!"

I will reveal the amusing result of this little talk later, but I was faintly aware as Doris was talking that her husband and manager for the last seventeen years, Marty Melcher, who kept dropping in and out on the interview, was slowly shaking his head.

At the time, Doris at 45 had become more than her famous girl-next-door image. She had given us extraordinary verve and fabulous dancing and singing, in *Calamity Jane* for instance, top comedy performances in films like *Pillow Talk*, and in her more mature years fine dramatic acting

in films like *The Man Who Knew Too Much* and *Love Me Or Leave Me* opposite James Cagney, when she played with shattering intensity the life
of early singer Ruth Etting, who had suffered from alcoholism and a
brutal husband. Now she was playing the married woman in films like
Please Don't Eat The Daisies and *Send Me No Flowers,* and soon she would
be playing the divorcee or the widow. While all this might seem a natural
progression, it was one that was shrewdly planned and master-minded
by husband Marty, and one that every girl star yearns for as they grow
older but very few achieve.

The most astonishing thing about Doris Day was that she achieved all
this against terrible odds, because ever since she was a child her life had
been criss-crossed with tragedies. Earlier, Doris had given me a unique
insight into some of those milestones in her life. She was born Doris
von Kappelhoff on 3 April 1924. Her father was a strict German music
teacher, who wanted her to become a classical musician like himself. Her
mother Alma wanted her to be a dancer.

When Doris was 12 her parents divorced, and to support Doris and
her older brother Paul, and pay for her daughter's dancing lessons, Alma
took a job in a bakery. The second tragedy came a year later, when Doris
had teamed up with a teenage boy dancer and they had their first work
in a touring show in Hamilton, Ohio. One night she was driven out by
a friend to buy some hamburgers. The road crossed the railway tracks in
the middle of the town, and their car was hit by a freight train. Doris's
right leg was crushed and broken in several places. For fourteen months
she lay in hospital, and doctors told her that her dreams of becoming a
fine dancer were over.

Still determined to make something of herself, Doris turned to singing, and again her mother paid for her lessons, this time by taking in
sewing. When Doris was 16, band leader Barney Rapp heard her sing
'Day After Day' on a local radio station and signed her up for his night
club. He felt it impossible to put the name Doris von Kappelhoff up in
lights so he dubbed her Doris Day, after the song, and the name stuck.
A stint with the Bob Crosby band took her to New York, where she was
soon snapped up by top band leader Les Brown at a much higher salary.
She repaid him by recording her first big hit, 'Sentimental Journey'.

When it seemed she was well on her way to become a top popular singer, she fell in love with Al Jorden, a young trombonist in the Jimmy Dorsey orchestra, and after their marriage he wanted her to give up her career.

"I was 17, and at the time I thought what I wanted most of all was a husband and family. But we discovered, because we had been travelling in different bands, we had never really known each other. I was really in love with his romantic letters, I suppose. Around them I'd fashioned a dream man, but he wasn't a dream – he was alive, young, and rather jealous. We were miserable right from the beginning. We had made a mistake."

Problems increased when Doris's son and only child Terry was born on 8 February 1942: after three months of trying to tour and take the child with them, Doris decided she could no longer subject her young baby to such a life, and went back to Cincinnati and her mother. She and Jorden were divorced in February 1943.

Doris then had to earn a living for three – herself, her mother and her son. Because the money was good, Doris went back on the road with the Les Brown band. She hated being parted from son Terry, but it was arranged that whenever Doris had a week-long gig, rather than one-night stands, her mother would take Terry to her.

For the next three years, travelling with the band, Doris seemed to be forever packing up and moving on. The boys in the band were protective – like brothers to her – but it was rare for a girl singer to marry one. However, Doris found herself becoming attracted to one of the musicians, George Weidler.

"He was witty and charming, and we were just good pals for about three years," she remembered. "Then the man he had replaced in the band came back from the Army. George went to California to try his luck down there … The minute we were separated, we fell in love, and I rushed to California to marry him."

For several months the couple lived in a trailer camp in Los Angeles, while George took what odd musician's jobs he could get. They were always short of money, and Doris, who now wanted just to be a housewife and provide a happy home for little Terry, had to go back to work again.

Through Hollywood agent Al Levy she was offered a lucrative engagement at the famous Little Club in New York, and George advised his wife to take it.

She had been in New York only a few days when a letter arrived from George Weidler saying that as far as he was concerned their marriage was over. "It was a terrible shock. It was the most awful thing that had ever happened to me," she recalled. "I just couldn't understand it."

Doris went into deep depression, unable to stop crying – the thought that she had failed yet again at being a good wife and mother was overwhelming. She wept before and after, and sometimes during, her appearances at the microphone, and the club's management were so worried they rang her agent for help. Al Levy, his hands full in Hollywood, sent up his junior partner, Marty Melcher. It wasn't the first time Marty had met Doris, but it was the first time he'd seen her so emotionally exposed. Her unhappiness aroused the instinctive kindness and understanding of people that, linked with his business acumen, was making him a much sought-after agent. Above all, he believed in her talent. One of his favourite records had been Doris singing 'Sentimental Journey'. As he once said, "I thought anyone who sings like that must be star material." But there was no romance between them for a long time. For years he was the patient man in the background, who fixed blown light fuses and cranky lawnmowers, did the weekend shopping, and was the man to whom Doris could pour out her troubles.

One night, hoping to be cheered up, she went to a party, where songwriters Jule Styne and Sammy Cahn remembered her from the Les Brown days and asked her to sing. They were so impressed they recommended her to director Michael Curtiz for his new film *It's Magic*, starring comedian Jack Carson. But during her audition for Curtiz Doris burst into tears again. "And what's more," she cried, ignoring agent Marty's alarmed shushings, "I can't act either. I've never acted in my life!"

Curtiz just laughed, and put a consoling arm round her shoulder. What he had wanted most of all was naturalness and honesty, and in Doris he had these qualities. He well knew, like everyone else in the business, that Doris was a gifted singer. As for her acting – well, he would solve that problem step by step. He signed her for the picture.

Then began for Doris the most exhausting phase of her life up to that point. She responded by working tirelessly, obsessively. Making good in the picture was only partly the reason. Only by sinking herself completely in her work could she take her mind away from the emptiness of her private life. By driving herself to exhaustion, she could at least return to her lonely hotel room at nights and find a little peace in sleep. She saw herself as a mother who rarely saw her son – a wife who'd failed twice at marriage before she was 25.

Looking back on this period, Doris told me: "It wasn't a pleasant time in my life. Both my marriages had failed. That was very disillusioning to me. I thought there must be something wrong with me, that I was not a good wife and perhaps couldn't be … I didn't know … I was so young. I was a bit conceited, I suppose, worrying about myself and my own reactions.

"I came into this business not thinking or caring about it very much. I was unhappy at the time. I was never very materially minded, and in a way it helped me forget about myself. It was very demanding work, and I wanted to see if I could do it well, match the challenge of it. But I was never terribly ambitious. I'm not ambitious now."

So, even in her first film, work was becoming a kind of therapy. What happened was the last thing Doris expected. *It's Magic* was a big hit. Doris, who'd never thought she would get to make a second film, emerged from it as Hollywood's newest girl star. A dizzy, gay and vivacious blonde who didn't have a care in her head. Warner Brothers began to star her in film after film. With her first pay cheque Doris brought Terry and her mother out to California, and they all moved into a pretty cottage in Hidden Valley outside Hollywood. For the first time she was living permanently with her son.

Her film success brought her big recording contracts and radio assignments. When she recorded 'It's Magic' in 1948 it soared over the million mark in a couple of weeks. Within two years of her first film Doris was earning $500,000 a year, which was high pay, even for a star in those days.

Now she was working under great pressure, and soon agent Al Levy had his hands so full, he delegated the *main* strings of her career to his former junior partner Marty, who was now spending more and more of his off-duty time with Doris. They got along well on this mutually platonic basis – as Marty had also suffered a broken marriage. They would joke with each other that perhaps, in their demanding world, happy and lasting marriage was a naive dream. Ever since the break-up of her second marriage Doris had been searching for a spiritual anchor, as was Marty.

It was their mutual discovery of Christian Science – oddly enough through a meeting with Doris's former husband George Weidler – that linked them closer together. One day George had rung up out of the blue asking to see Doris, and she had been amazed at the transformation in him – he was completely happy, and at peace with himself. He explained in detail to Doris what he had found in his new religion.

"That was how it really all began for Marty and me," Doris told me. "It was the turning point in my life. It wasn't just a lot of talk. It was *doing*. Here was a living example of something fine. George was *being* all he believed. I went back and told Marty all about it, and the wonderful thing was he understood completely, because we both needed what George had found."

Any final doubts about marriage were removed on the day that Doris's young son Terry, who liked Marty immensely, came up to his mother in their kitchen and suggested outright that she should marry Marty. They tied the knot quietly in a local justice of the peace office on 3 April 1951, Doris's twenty-seventh birthday.

In a new, larger house in Toluca Lake the couple began a clean-living lifestyle. Doris gave up smoking, and they kept an ice cream and soda fountain in their living room – no alcoholic drinks at all. They didn't go to smart parties, or give them. And much of her subsequent success and rise to superstardom was due to her downright perseverance. She forced herself to take up dancing lessons again. The muscles of her right leg – injured in that car crash ten years earlier – gave her a great deal of pain at first, but she persevered. The crash might have damaged her leg, but it certainly hadn't sapped her will. In *Calamity Jane* one is immediately struck by her tremendous verve. No girl star since has ever outshone her for sheer perky vitality. Much of this radiance came from the simple and uncomplicated life that she established very early with Marty.

"I don't dissipate," she told me. "I need all my energy for my work. It's so easy in Hollywood to fall into the celebrity trap, so easy to start living up to the expected image. I've seen lovely, talented people ruin their careers and jeopardise their private lives because they couldn't say no to a thousand parties, couldn't say no to an accelerated career that didn't leave them free to be a wife or a husband … couldn't say no to a life which seemed glamorous but proved hazardous."

Doris would not do personal appearances, and felt no desire to accept any of the hugely lucrative engagements she was constantly being offered in Las Vegas cabaret. That kind of work reminded her too much of the unhappy times in her life – those lonely one-night stands with the bands of her youth. She hated to live up to any 'star' image. She was a familiar sight in Beverly Hills when she cycled to do her own shopping, and waved and called out to her neighbours. I even photographed her myself on one of these trips. "I really enjoy it," she told me. "Most people forget how much fun it is to ride a bicycle. Anyway, I have to shop so often, as I forget little things." It made her a sitting duck for autograph hunters, but she didn't mind that.

I must say that I very much liked some of her philosophy for living, just as I'd been impressed by that of Cary Grant, which I wrote about in my first volume of autobiography.* When I asked how the deep, understanding love she and Marty knew had been achieved, Doris replied, "We strove to learn more about ourselves, and what the real meaning of the word 'love' was – to have a better understanding of each other.

"The only way you can really do that with another person is to know your own faults and work on them. And I mean *really* work on them, because we are always pointing the finger at the other person and saying 'You, you are wrong.' But it's *not* the other person; everything starts within one's own consciousness. How one feels about someone else is right within oneself, you see. When you become a better person and strive to improve yourself, you'll find the other person is improving too. I don't know quite how it happens, but it just does. One has to work on oneself, try to be better. That's the big thing … I know I have a long way to go."

---

* *My Wicked First Life.*

At another time I asked her how she would feel if her career suddenly went wrong, and she lost everything she now possessed?

"I think I'd just get up and start all over again. It wouldn't change me, though it might change my circumstances temporarily. It wouldn't bother me too much if I were suddenly broke tomorrow. No, that's why you have to build your house on a rock. I mean your mental, spiritual house. If you do that, no change in material circumstances can really change or hurt you."

Doris didn't like to dwell on the idea that her personal life had been unusually tough. "Everybody has it tough somewhere along the line, I think," she told me. "Everybody has a sad story in their lives. I really believe that no matter what happens to you, in the long run it always works out for the best. You may find it hard to believe at the time, though. I have never plotted or planned my life. I really believe that if we stay out of it, let things happen, and just pray for guidance and direction, then we are led to do the right things by that higher power we call God."

Doris and Marty's marriage was unique in that not only had they been happily married for seventeen years in a town where over eighty-five per cent of star marriages foundered in divorce, but their *esprit* together helped them found their enormously successful business empire. I asked Doris if she could have achieved as much without Marty's help.

"No … I think Martin and I are extremely compatible. The main thing is we thought along the same lines, we liked the same things, and our goals were the same. And it had nothing to do with money. You see, money was incidental to us. We never made money our god. And we never would. If you make a god out of anything material then you're finished, just useless. The creative impulse, the real creative drive dies. The work itself is the object, the activity itself, not the rewards. They should come incidentally."

She seemed embarrassed when I told her that, out of all the major women stars I had interviewed in the past twelve years, she seemed the least spoiled. "I think it's very important to stay a woman," she smiled. "If you let yourself become hard and driving, you lose your femininity. I always liked to do the cooking and cleaning in the house. I've never had live-in help in my life. I'm just not the hard-driving type."

It was at the end of our interview that Doris asked me whether I'd done any acting, and suggested they should give me a film test. I was vaguely aware that Marty was slowly shaking his head. As I thanked Doris and walked away, I hadn't quite reached the door when I heard Marty hiss to Doris: "No! His eyes are too close together!"

Needless to say, I never expected to hear any more about any film test, but not only because of anything Marty had said. A few days after my interview, although he had given no indication that he was unwell, Marty became ill and was taken into hospital. All Hollywood was shocked two days later when the news media blazoned the fact of his death from an unsuspected heart condition.

Doris, who had just started work on her own TV sitcom series, was devastated. One of her close friends told me: "She's absolutely destroyed. She's completely torn apart. For once her belief in positive thinking seems to have let her down." But within a few days of grieving, Doris emerged with a brave smile for the world. The TV series had been Marty's own pet project. The TV networks were relying on her show to replace the very popular *I Love Lucy*, and had invested record sums in it. And Doris also knew that the livings of scores of other people depended on her going back to work and on the show's success – and the show's success depended on Doris Day. She did not let them down.

The strange truth is that we see more of Doris Day now than we saw of her in her prime. Her films are on TV many times a year, not just the one or two times when we went to see her in our old movie cinemas. And some thirty-seven years after our interview I still derive occasional amusing moments. When I'm shaving, I sometimes grimace at my mirror image and hiss: "Your eyes are too close together!"

9

The Wild One

I had been trying to get him for weeks, but always his studios and agent said he was out of town. Needing to get something good on the dynamic, charismatic star who often diced with death in fast cars or on motorbikes in his *real* life, I had, two weeks ago, managed to get a very interesting interview with his beautiful wife, Neile. But now, as I walked into my favourite bar of the Raincheck Club on Sunset Strip, there he was: Steve McQueen.

He was sitting in a corner niche with a couple of pals. Obviously, it wouldn't be wise to just walk up to them, so I went to the bar nearby. Two beers later, and someone was standing beside me ordering more beers, and chatting to the young girl serving at the bar. It was *him*! Heart now pounding, I managed to grab his attention by saying that I was a writer and had recently had lunch with his wife. The sudden scowl on his face softened when I hastily explained that I was working for top women's magazines in Britain, Europe and Canada, as well as the *Daily Mail* group in London, and one of my main assignments was to try and get a meaningful interview with *him*. I added the white lie that I had just driven down specially from the wilds of Canada

"The wilds of Canada? I did a bit of logging in BC. What are you doing up there?"

"Well, I was a logger too. And I built a log cabin on a wild sea cliff, where I'm writing a novel."

"You have a woman with you?"

When I said no, he asked, "Don't you get lonesome out there?"

"Well, I am trying to create, but some of the time I *do* get lonely, yeah."

"How do you cope with it?"

I replied, somewhat pompously: "Well, I figure unless you can master loneliness you can never master yourself." Steve thought a second or two, said "Wow." (He'd had a few more drinks than me, I thought.) Then he suggested that maybe I didn't like women. I replied that I loved them. And through my job in the past I'd met and had much loving with some of the world's most famous and beautiful. I mentioned a few names.

"So why isolate yourself out there in Canada?"

"I'm trying to escape my past, turn it into something better, write a fine novel."

Steve suddenly banged his hand on the counter, glared at me with those large, electric blue eyes, and said "Hell! Man, *you* can come out to the house ... I wanna talk to you again." He gave me his address and told me the time to visit in two days' time, a Saturday. I said his wife might think it odd, after my chat with her, if I turned up at their house. "She won't be there," said Steve. "She's away for a weekend break to our place in Palm Springs. Now I gotta go back to my pals." He turned away with a beer in each hand, and asked the bar girl to deliver the third one.

Next day I went through my research notes on McQueen and my lunch talk with Neile. I recalled her telling me, "When Steve finishes a picture, he feels he should rest a month or two, but he can't just sit down, watch TV or read a book. He gets very restless, because he *needs* to work. Sometimes he wakes me up in the middle of the night and says, 'Let's go to the house at Palm Springs.' So we take one of the motorbikes and off we go. As soon as we get there, he says, 'Let's go home.'!"

Neile McQueen laughed when she talked like this about her husband. She knew that this was just how most people imagined him to be from his films – restless, moody, temperamental, a one-time problem boy who had finally made good in Hollywood, and yet a man who still lived life to the hilt, and to hell with the consequences. It was an image that had made Steve McQueen almost unique as a male star, one that women could adore and men could identify with. His on-screen personality was explosive: the piercing blue eyes, a nose that had been busted in three fights, the body honed by a restless energy – a Humphrey Bogart with spark plugs.

In real life, too, he was an extraordinary mixture. His youth was unhappy: he never knew his father, and at 14 his mother and stepfather sent him to a home for wayward boys. Afterwards he worked as a deckhand on an oil tanker, as a carpenter, a carnival barker, an oil driller, a logger in Canada, a TV repair man and even, at 16, a runner for a brothel in the Dominican Republic after he jumped a ship. If now, at 38, he still needed a sense of danger in his life – he did his own dangerous stunt-driving, such as in those hair-raising car-chase sequences in *Bullitt* – one could perhaps excuse him.

Neile told me that, when Steve competed, it was mostly against himself. "Some days he just takes off across the desert on one of his powerful bikes – he needs to re-create danger in his life, to feel he is somehow master of his own fate. He likes to capture the feeling of danger with a fast machine – so danger itself becomes *his* captive. He feels closer to reality somehow. It's not a death wish – some men just *have* to be on a tightrope sometimes."

Neile, however, also revealed a completely different side to her husband behind the tough public image – the strong devoted family man: "As wild as he is, he is very, very square as far as the children and I are concerned. Almost puritanical in fact. I think that's mostly because of his own unhappy youth.

"He has calmed down a lot from the really wild man I first married. He's a marvellous father, is very fair with the children, and doesn't spoil them. And he has this thing about my cooking. Although we have a small staff at home he doesn't like anyone else's cooking but mine. It's flattering – but sometimes I wish he'd let me employ a cook now and then." She laughed, an infectious laugh: "And he's a very jealous man. If he thought I'd actually been out with someone else he'd kill me. It wouldn't be instant divorce. It would be instant death!"

At this time Neile had been happily married to Steve for thirteen years. It seemed he had found in her the emotional security, the spiritual anchor he'd needed to escape the bitter wandering days of his youth, to get where he was at the top of the film tree. Then my research also revealed that he was no mere celluloid hero. He had represented America in motor cycle trials in Europe and, with Stirling Moss, had been a paid member of the BMC car-racing team at Sebring in Florida. I was certainly looking forward to meeting him again.

When I arrived at his palatial home, atop a small mountain in Brentwood, Los Angeles, I soon understood why it was known as The Castle. It was a huge, Spanish-style house with a red-tiled roof, and it overlooked a great crescent bay of the Pacific Ocean, and the pinks, greys and greens of the houses and gardens of Beverly Hills and Hollywood. Steve and Neile had chosen it for its complete privacy. A ten-foot-high wall surrounded the three-acre grounds, which contained a private swimming pool.

Driving my old milk truck/camper up the long, broad driveway, the McQueen passion for the outdoor life was immediately obvious. Next to the gleaming burgundy Ferrari and Neile's dark-green Excalibur (a tenth wedding anniversary present from Steve) and her sports Mustang were six motorcycles, two of them caked in mud. An underslung Jaguar SS, which McQueen called 'the old green rat', lurked in the dark of a garage. A dust-encrusted pickup truck half blocked the driveway, and next to that was the smart McQueen motor caravan. (I parked my disreputable-looking truck as far away from it as possible.) On the lawn by the house stood a little red-and-white fire truck belonging to Steve's eight-year-old son, Chad. Right by it was a large dolls' pram – the property of daughter Terry, aged nine and a half.

I came to a massive, arched oak door, stated who I was into an electric buzzer, and the door swung open silently. A sudden movement to my right, and there was Steve McQueen. He greeted me with a big smile, crushed my hand in an iron grip, took me into an elegant but informal living room, cracked open a tin of San Miguel beer, handed it to me, sat down, and cracked one open for himself.

The interview that followed was both long and fascinating, and there is no room for it all here, save a few extracts. I asked him why he liked to race bikes and cars in his personal life, and he put it this way: "Around the studios now, practically everybody waits on me. They powder my nose, and tell me what they think I want to hear. After a while you could become convinced you're a superman.

"But when you're racing a motorcycle the man on the next bike doesn't give a damn who you are. If he beats you, it means he's a better man than you are, and he's not afraid to tell you you're lousy. Racing keeps my equilibrium intact, man. It makes it hard for me to believe I'm some great cat or God's gift to humanity."

I found that he was still ultra-sensitive about the more painful areas of his boyhood, yet I discovered he was now endowing the home for wayward boys he had been sent to – the Junior Boys' Republic in Chino, California (from which he at first ran away but was taken back and stayed on to finish ninth grade) with a yearly scholarship for the most promising student. Three times a year he visited the boys there. He was also serving with leading city dignitaries on the Advisory Council for Youth Studies at the University of Southern California. Twice a year he took clothing and medical supplies to the impoverished Navajo Indians on a reservation in Arizona. "It's not entirely unselfish work," he smiled. "I love to run my truck down there, go into their homes and talk to them, and sleep outside for a few nights. They don't see movies, so they don't know who I am. And they have a saying I like very much – 'A land where there is time enough and room enough.'"

Steve told me that at the end of his life he would like to be known as a man of compassion, with a strong sense of justice, and a zestful love for life. "I want to be like that, not just for myself, my wife and kids," he told me, "but because somewhere, right now, there are kids going through what I went through. Maybe if they know I survived they might find hope. I can't say they'll ever forget what's happening to them if they're being badly treated, but if they hold out they'll get through okay and learn to live with bad memories – still learn to love.

"I'm a gambler by nature, but I don't believe you can get anywhere in life unless you have a fixed goal in mind, and are willing to take chances to achieve what you want. But you have to work hard to attract luck to your side."

After a long interview, in which Steve threw fascinating light on some of the crucial stages in his life, we went outside and began fooling about with one of his chainsaws (known as power saws in America and

Canada). He took me to a pile of logs and asked me how I tackled cutting off the right-sized 'bolts' to chop up into firewood. I hauled the top log out so that it overhung the edge of the pile, and couldn't pinch the saw towards the end of the cut. Then I took the Stihl saw from him, tugged the starter cord twice, and cut off a couple of foot-long bolts, easy to chop up. Steve took the saw from me and did the same, and he was very good. He could handle a power saw okay.

I then recalled a cute trick I'd learned in Canada from a top veteran faller. I said: "When you are falling a tree, you now and then need a wedge, to help tip it. Right?" He said, "Yes." I said, "If you don't happen to have a tree wedge with you, do you know how to make one?" He said "No."

I saw that one of the thicker logs was lying, upraised and trapped in by two other logs, in the untidy pile. I got the saw up to almost full revs and ploughed it into the butt end at an angle until I'd cut in about a foot. Then, keeping the saw at the same high revs I applied an opposite cut three inches from the first and at an angle that would form the wedge. Then I cut through top and bottom, stopped the saw, prised out the neat wedge with the tip of an axe blade, and handed it to Steve.

"Hey, that's real neat! I'll try it too." He did, but when the tip of the saw hit the log, it jumped upwards. And it did a second time. The expression on Steve's face told me he was *not* pleased. I told him the secret was to get the saw going hard, almost at full revs, and to keep it that way throughout all the cutting. And he had to hold it hard, too. He tried again, and finally mastered the technique. He then looked at me with what I *thought* was new respect; then he said: "Can you ride a bike?"

I said yes, and that at one time I'd been a successful amateur racing cyclist. Steve looked momentarily puzzled, then it dawned on him. "No, I don't mean a pushbike, a pedal bike. I mean a real *bike*!" And he indicated the two mud-encrusted motorbikes near the pickup truck, which was also half caked in mud. I told him I had ridden a bike, but not for a long time, not for some twenty years. "What was your last bike?" I told him the feeble truth – that it had been a BSA Bantam, which had only a two-stroke engine and couldn't be coaxed over fifty miles an hour.

"Sounds a loada crap!" he said. He told me that when he was in serious training, like when he practised for the famous motorcycling scenes in *The Great Escape*, he took a three- or four-day trip to the Mojave Desert with one or two like-minded pals, camped out, and gave the bikes a real hard go. But he did know of a fairly good, deserted spot in the Santa Monica Mountains, north of Hollywood, and if I fancied a go we could take bikes up there right now! The prospect of riding motor cycles with Steve McQueen was an adventure far too good to miss, but I also had to try and quell a slight feeling of fear.

We manhandled the two motorbikes up the sloping tailgate of the truck, and were soon bowling north along the San Diego Freeway. Bowling? We were speeding, and Steve drove fast, expertly, and took a few chances I'd not have taken. As I took sideways looks at him I recalled an amusing anecdote his wife Neile had given me: "He was really wild when we first met," she had said. "I'd never been exposed to all the things he exposed me to, like motorbikes and speed. On our first date in New York we flew up one avenue and down another. 'Do you always run around town like this?' I asked him. 'Not always,' he said. 'Sometimes I'm actually going some place!'"

We reached Steve's chosen spot – a large, deserted and desert-like area that contained small hillocks and patches of brush and hard sand. Steve showed me how the clutch, throttle and gears worked, and told me to try the manoeuvres he was making but to take it easy at first – to get used to the machine in my own time.

Well, I can only say I was licked! Thrashed! I might have matched him on the chain saw, but I was no match for him on a bike. The first time I gingerly let the clutch out, the powerful machine shot off so fast it nearly disappeared from between my legs; I just managed to hastily throttle down and cling on. Some of my old skills came back, like when you ride a pushbike after a long lay-off, and eventually I managed some credible swerve-stops, sending up showers of sand.

Steve was soon speeding up the hillocks and jumping his bike further and further, but the first time I tried to emulate him – a lot more slowly – my front wheel was not quite in the bike line, but was slightly turned to the right. The bike crashed when it hit the ground, and I was sent sprawling to the left. Luckily, I was unhurt, apart from small cuts and bruises, and I got back on the bike and finally managed a few successful jumps, but a lot smaller than Steve's.

At the end of our session Steve slid to a sand-spraying stop beside me, and said, "Well, for a guy who's not been on a bike for twenty years, and a crap bike at that, you're not too bad, not too bad at all."

What a compliment! But I felt I had to tell him the whole truth, and said: "Well, before the crap bike, and many years ago, I was a dispatch rider in the British Army!"

Before we parted, Steve paid me the biggest compliment of all, saying he would love to visit me in my isolated cliff-top cabin in Canada and do some serious fishing. But this never happened, for soon after this he was fully involved in the most ambitious project of his life, the film *Le Mans*. When the film eventually became a critical and box office failure, Steve had felt broken – and never raced again. Besides all that, after my next and last interview with the greatest movie star of all, I left Canada.

10

Big Man — Biggest Star

My meeting with John Wayne, the most popular movie star the world has ever known, was bizarre. I had just driven down from my wilderness outpost in Canada in the old milk truck I had converted into a camper van, and was on the outdoor set of the film *The Undefeated* in Baton Rouge, Louisiana. Shooting was over for the day, and they were all having a few drinks on small tables – the actors, the cameramen, the grips and the electricians. Suddenly the publicity man said, "I'll introduce you to Mr Wayne now." My heart pounded faster as I was led to one of the tables.

To my surprise, a huge but totally *bald* man rose to his feet to envelope my hand with at first a soft grip, then a quick hard grip, as if to say a friendly "Hello" then a warning "Take care!" It was a few seconds before I could perceive the familiar Wayne features under the bald pate. He looked like a giant version of Grock, the famous Victorian clown. He really was big, a full 6 feet 4½ inches tall, and at 244 pounds he had put back all the weight he had lost in his brush with cancer, when most of his left lung had been removed in an operation three years earlier. He pulled up a chair, told me to sit, and handed me a large glass of tequila. Luckily, I had become used to tequila on my trip round Mexico a year earlier, when covering preparations for the 1968 Olympics for the *Daily Express* and magazines in Australia and South Africa.

I tried to keep up with the talk, the tall stories, and drinking with Wayne, feeling as I had when at the age of 16 my father had challenged me to 'join the men' when he had brought a party of Canadian airmen back to our house for drinks and a New Year's Eve card-playing party. I'd kept drinking with those men then, between visits to the loo to throw up, and never touched alcohol again until I was 22! I have always believed that first 'shock' to my liver must have prepared it for later alcoholic onslaught, for I've been able to hold my own with anyone in the drinks department ever since. And for a world-travelling show business reporter that was rather important.

By the time the end-of-shooting party with Wayne had finished, he, a key grip, the main cameraman and myself seemed to be the only men still talking any sense. As he got up to leave, Wayne looked at the camera-man and said, "If a goddam Limey can drink well with us, he may be worth talking to!" Then he winked at me, jabbed a giant forefinger gently into my solar plexus, and said, "Grab me every time I finish a shot or you see me walking back to my trailer. Stay close! I won't come for you – you have to come and get *me*."

I promised to do my best, walked back to my milk truck camper, which was parked below trees a few hundred yards off the film set, and climbed into my rickety plywood bed. I found it hard to get to sleep, worrying about what faced me tomorrow. I had almost run out of money after finishing my 'great novel' and studying the dramatic bears and wild-life in the Canadian wilds, but *Woman* magazine in Britain had offered me the princely sum of £3,000 if I could get a good three-part series out of Wayne, especially if I could also speak to his wife and angle it from her point of view. Top magazines in Germany, France and Australia had also shown interest. But there was more to it than financial reward: not only was John Wayne the world's top box office star, and had been for many years, but he had also been part of my life. He had ridden through the dreams of my boyhood and youth, as he may have done through yours, his films almost part of real experience. The tough, laconic, decent-at-heart Ringo Kid in *Stagecoach*, seeking to revenge his father's murder; the outspoken, rebellious western sons of the early 1940s who'd grow up straight, provided they didn't get shot first.

By the late 1940s Wayne was already the father figure, the head scout or trail boss to a bunch of wild saddle tramps, or the lone big man on a big horse, hard and merciless with men who stepped out of line but shy with women, treating them with rough backwoods courtesy. Where had he come from, before the mountains and the long grass? We all wanted to know. His face was the great American face – tough, friendly, completely masculine. He never made a film of salacious sex, or played an anti-hero. He sold sincerity all the way down the line, nearly always the rugged champion who helped the underdog and who served the cause of justice – single-handed if necessary. He conveyed great emotional strength, his films tending to glorify the eternal physical and emotional verities that most people believe make life finer – friendship, loyalty, integrity, love, and the eventual triumph of good over evil. To millions of filmgoers, in whose lives good and evil often waged inconclusive battles, John Wayne's constant portrayals of tough goodness were not only fine entertainment but also personally reassuring. They still are!*

I woke early, and as I was going through my mass of research notes and prepared questions I became lost in reverie, my mind's eye reliving some scenes from his finest films: the homesick young sailor in *The Long Voyage Home*; the unstable but honest sea dog in *Reap The Wild Wind*; his star personality finding new fields in war films like *Flying Tigers*, and *The Fighting Seabees*; skippering the little torpedo boats in *They Were Expendable*, with the Japanese shells falling dangerously close; red-scarved and bawling orders from the deck in *Wake Of The Red Witch*; or the dignified, ageing cattleman in *Red River*, when Hollywood chiefs first realised he had become a very good actor.

The following year, 1949, he made the classic *She Wore A Yellow Ribbon*, when he played an ageing cavalry officer trying to defeat the Indians amassing for General Custer's last stand. By now he had been voted the world's most popular box office star, a position he held until long after his death. He next played the big, tough sergeant bullying his rookie marines into manhood in *Sands Of Iwo Jima*, when he was first nominated for an Oscar.

---

* The truth is we see far *more* of John Wayne movies today than we ever did during his prime, when he seldom made more than two films in a year. During the festive period of 22 December to 2 January 2008, as I write this, there were *twelve* Wayne movies shown on our TV networks.

In my mind's eye I saw again the 'green ould sod' of Ireland, where in *The Quiet Man* he had gone seeking peace from tragic pugilistic memories, only to find himself romancing Maureen O'Hara and fighting the screen's greatest-ever fist fight with his real-life pal, the late, lovable Victor McLaglen. "Oh, 'tis the Marquis o' Queensbury rules is it?" roars McLaglen, belting Wayne before he's back on his feet, and off they go again, battling through bars and down the mountain side till that final lusty victory when all are pals and Wayne gets his girl.

I recalled, too, his convincing performance in the epic western *The Searchers*, where he played harsh, embittered rancher Ethan Edwards, who returns from chasing cattle rustlers to find his brother's family wiped out in a Comanche raid and his two young daughters abducted by the Indians. The search and personal vendetta dragged on for years, and despite Edwards' rigid, unbending nature Wayne brilliantly conveyed the man's tragic loneliness. I had loved his change of style, too, in *Rio Bravo*, where he was a sheriff who had single-handedly to defend a town against an outlaw band. He extracted as much in comedy as Gary Cooper had in drama in *High Noon*. Where Cooper pleaded for help from the townsfolk but finally didn't need it, Wayne refused help but ultimately had to depend on it.

I remembered some of his top action roles, such as in *Hatari* where he played a big-game hunter, rode in bucking, open Land Rovers over the rough terrain and, refusing to use stuntmen, threw slings round the necks of running rhinos himself. And of course his up and at 'em role as the battling general in *The Longest Day*. I particularly liked his fabulous comedy/drama performance in *El Dorado*, where he and his old pal Robert Mitchum hammed it up as ageing gunfighter and drunken sheriff who join forces against ruthless range barons.

The upward surge into comedy had culminated at this time in his flawless portrait of the flawed sheriff Rooster Cogburn in *True Grit*, for which he finally won the Oscar. "Rooster was the kind of marshal the screen had never seen before," he said at the time; "an old, sloppy-looking, hard-drinking, disreputable, one-eyed sonofabitch who'd been around long enough to know you don't fool around with outlaws, but use every trick in the book, fair or foul, to bring 'em to justice. A mean old bastard, just like me! I couldn't wait to play him."

Before *True Grit*, Wayne produced, directed and starred in his most controversial film, *The Green Berets*, in which he wanted to show audiences just what US soldiers were going through in the Vietnam war. American liberals and critics accused him of glorifying an unpopular war. "Glorifying an unpopular war?" he retorted. "What war was ever popular, for God's sake?" He proved his point when the film made $8,000,000 in the first three months of its release.

This was the movie giant I had come to interview, and when I approached him after his first scene next morning I was very relieved that he not only remembered me, but also greeted me with a big smile. He was now wearing one of the kinds of hairpiece he always wore in his films. When I was explaining I wanted to tell a *little* of his life story, especially his early life and struggles, he put up a huge hand: "Hold on," he said. "Why should I tell *you* my story? A lot of folk have been after it."

I replied, "Well, it won't be that long ... er, I won't stay long. And it will be accurate ... er ..."

"Oh yes?"

"And you can check it too, for accuracy ..."

Wayne was still glaring. "Give me another reason!"

I couldn't think of another one, so I just stammered, "Er, well, I need the money!"

There was a pregnant pause, and I feared I'd blown it at the start. Then Wayne gave a loud laugh, pointed to me, and said, "Oh, *you* need the money! Now that *is* a good reason! What do you wanna know?"

From that moment on big John Wayne was more cooperative than any star I'd ever met. He let me get to him in nearly every spare moment over two whole days, even inviting me to lunch with him privately in his luxury trailer, and he seemed oddly flattered that I had done full research. Early on in our meetings it became clear to me why Wayne had become the believable mythical Homeric hero, the very personification of the West. As I teased the story of his life from him, piecemeal, it became obvious that he actually did come from real pioneer stock. He was born Marion Michael Morrison on 26 May 1907 in the small town of

Winterset, Iowa, where his father, of Scots-Irish descent, ran a small, old-fashioned chemists shop. 'Doc' Morrison handled minor first aid cases himself, and handed out prescriptions along with his own homespun philosophy, from which he gave his son three rules for living:

1. Always keep your word.
2. A gentleman never insults anyone intentionally.
3. Don't look for trouble. But if you get into a fight, make sure you win it.

Wayne laughed as he recalled that he didn't agree with the second one. "A gentleman never insults anyone unintentionally. If you do, it has to be for a good reason."

Doc Morrison was very popular, and could never press his many friends for prompt payment of their bills, so by the time Wayne was six years old, Doc was almost insolvent. He also developed severe lung congestion, and his doctor told him to move to a warmer climate. Doc moved the family out west, but being a late arrival in 1913, he had a tough time finding good land, and had to settle for a small, eighty-acre ranch near Palmdale, on the edge of the arid Mojave desert. Doc and young Wayne worked together, sometimes fourteen hours a day, clearing sage brush and planting corn and peas.

"We were real homesteaders," Wayne told me. "Rattlesnakes? We killed 'em by the hundreds. I saw so many as a kid they meant nothing. In the end, apart from not actually treading on them, we ignored them. But jackrabbits were our real enemy. I remember my dad planted five acres of black-eyed peas, and we went out one morning and they were showing up nice and green, about half an inch high. We went out again next day and there wasn't a bit of green left. The rabbits had cleared the lot in one night. Can you imagine how many rabbits that took?"

They were hard, rough days for his parents, but to Wayne, a strong boy from all the physical work, they were merely adventurous. To get to school eight miles away Wayne rode the family's only horse, a mare called Jenny, and twice a week he picked up the family groceries from the general store in Lancaster and strapped them across the horse's back along with his school books. When Jenny caught a serious disease and had to be put down it hit young Wayne hard. "It was my first emotional tragedy," he told me. "It's one reason why I now only employ wranglers who love and truly care for their horses."

After two more years Doc Morrison had to admit defeat, and Wayne's mother, Molly, persuaded him the sterile Mojave desert had won. They moved down to Glendale, then a small town outside Los Angeles. Doc went back to his old trade and got work in a pharmacy. Two more years and Doc again bought his own drug store, but money was still scarce, so at the age of 12 Wayne had a newspaper round and delivered his dad's medicines to help pay his own upkeep. The family lived next door to the local cinema, so by delivering the theatre's show bills with his papers, Wayne could see all the new movies free. He was fascinated by the old cowboy stars like William S. Hart, Hoot Gibson and Tom Mix, but when he played at movies with other kids on the block he did not imitate any of them.

"I imitated Douglas Fairbanks Senior! I admired his duelling, his stunts and agility, his fearlessness in the face of danger and his cheeky grin when about to kiss the girl!"

It was, and still is, a common belief that Wayne was referred to as 'The Duke' in Hollywood. He was not. He was known as just 'Duke'. He was called Duke Wayne, not John Wayne, in the business, as well as by his family and friends. He told me how he got the name. "Our family had a large Airedale dog called Duke. Often, when I walked to Glendale High School, I would take him with me and leave him at the fire station, then pick him up again on the way home. The firemen knew the dog's name but not mine, so they dubbed me 'Little Duke'. When I started pushing six feet in height they dropped the 'Little'!"

Wayne became an honours student at Glendale High, president of the senior school, and a star football player. Disappointed at not getting into the US Naval Academy at Annapolis (although he had come fourth among thirty applicants), he capitalised on his athletic prowess and entered the University of Southern California on a football scholarship. To pay his way he worked as a map plotter, as a football ticket salesman, and then as a props man at 20th Century Fox studios. Wayne grinned as he told me how he met the legendary director John 'Jack' Ford, for whom years later he was to star in some of the finest films ever made.

"He was making an Irish movie, *Mother Machree*, and was a props man short. He had made a huge outdoor set of a rural scene, and to give it a more authentic touch he had a large flock of geese there. Most of the time the geese weren't needed, but they didn't know that, and waddled all over the place, into the cameras and up the artificial mountain. So my first job on a John Ford picture was as a gooseherder! I didn't mind one bit – I'd never been paid so much for doing so little!"

During a break in shooting, Ford, a tough, powerful man himself, challenged Wayne to a football tackle. Wayne, who was then playing in the USC football team, the best on the West Coast, was fed up with people asking him to show them how he got down into the guard position.

"How could I show them? I wasn't really busting into anyone. But I got down on all fours, and braced myself so Ford could push and pull me a little and have his moment of fun. But Ford had played ball himself, and he suddenly lit out and kicked my arms from under me, so I went flat on my face, in the plaster mud, in front of everyone.

"That got me mad, so I said, quietly, 'Let's try that again.' Ford charged, went to dodge round me. But I whirled and hit him right across the chest, dumping him heavily on his backside. There was a deadly silence, as Ford was highly respected, if not feared, and I thought, 'Hell, I've just charged myself right out of the picture business.' But Ford just sat there a few moments in shocked surprise, then threw back his head and roared with laughter, and everyone on the set joined in."

It was the start of one of the most profound friendships in Wayne's life, one still enduring at the time I met him. Ford got him jobs as a props man, and gave him bit parts. His first semi-starring role was in *The Big Trail* for director Raoul Walsh, but it was made with the new 70 mm Grandeur process, and was far ahead of its time. To show it, cinemas had to buy a bigger screen and special lenses to fit onto their projectors, and in the Depression of the 1930s few could afford the extra expense. Wayne told me: "The poverty was incredible. They were busting up boxes and making fires in the streets to keep warm, selling apples from their gardens for eating money. Ruined men were leaping from high windows, and it was no time for fancy innovations in the movies." It was the only film Wayne made that lost money.

For the next *nine* years Wayne plugged along in a series of B westerns, which he admitted were "pretty dreadful", but he was learning his trade, even doing a lot of stuntwork, and along with ex-rodeo champion turned stuntman Yakima Canutt, he actually invented the modern bar room brawling techniques of throwing-murderous looking punches that do untold damage to thin air: the blow narrowly misses, and the sound of the punch is added to the soundtrack later.

"It wasn't that we were such great inventive geniuses. We raced through film after film with such speed that if we'd carried on the old system, where actors actually hit each other's shoulders, we'd have been eternally black and blue."

Wayne told me some hilarious stories of those early films and stunt-work, and how he and other lovers of spirited horseplay in spare time got together to have boisterous fun. The group known fondly – and some-times not so fondly – as Jack Ford's Rolling Stock Company included pals such as Ward Bond, Yakima Canutt, Grant Withers and Johnny (Tarzan) Weismuller. These big, beefy guys frolicked so vigorously that the club-house of the Hollywood Athletic Club is said to have borne the scars for years.

Once, when on a wild duck shoot, Wayne's shotgun accidentally went off and peppered Ward Bond's backside. As the shots were being removed at the local hospital, Wayne quipped: "Well, I just wanted to see what pat-tern the pellets made at forty yards!"

Wayne revealed that after ten years as an actor he felt he was in a rut, and wanted to give up playing the B western heroes; but he had a wife – Panamanian diplomat's daughter Josephine Saenz – and their four children to support, so he carried on. He was following Ford's constant friendly advice: "Get all the experience you can, in anything you can get. Just keep getting plenty of screen time."

One day, Ford invited Wayne onto his yacht for drinks, and showed him a terrific short story for which he had just bought the screen rights. Wayne read it and knew it would be a winner, with all the great Bret Harte western characters in it, and a strong story line. "We discussed it for a while; then Jack asked me who he could get to play the lead in it. I'd just seen a fine performance by Lloyd Nolan, so I said 'Heck, I know the right guy – Lloyd Nolan.' Jack groaned, and said, 'Oh, darn you, Duke. Can't *you* do it?' I nearly dropped my drink with surprise! And for nearly four years I went around with bated breath because Jack couldn't find a producer who would accept me, then known only as a B western actor, in the lead role as the Ringo Kid."

Ford stuck to his belief in Wayne until top producer Walter Wanger agreed to back him. The film, finally called *Stagecoach*, was the great classic western of its time. It won three Academy Awards, revolutionised the whole western film genre, and elevated Duke Wayne to stardom. No wonder that for the next twenty years or more, whenever Jack Ford wanted Wayne for a picture, the only question Wayne asked was: "What hat, which door, and when do I come in?"

Wayne went from film to film, with barely a week off in between, and unfortunately in that time his first marriage failed, although the couple remained friends, and Wayne continued a solicitous interest in and financial backing for his ex-wife and their four children. A second marriage, to tempestuous Mexican actress Esperanza Baur, who was unable to have children, also failed. By the time I met him, on location near Baton Rouge, Wayne had been married to the beautiful Peruvian actress Pilar Palette for fifteen years, and they had three children of their own.

Once I knew I had the best of his personal story in my notebooks, I waited until a good moment during our second day's lunch in his trailer to pop the question I had been dreading most of all – would he mind if, to get a woman's perspective, I interviewed his wife? He thought a few moments, then to my amazement slapped his huge thigh and said, "What a helluva good idea! If Pilar agrees." Later in the afternoon Duke came over to where I was standing and handed me a piece of paper with the address of his Newport Beach home on it, plus its telephone number. He said that because it was nearly a 2,000-mile drive from Baton Rouge, and my truck must be slow, he had arranged for me to meet Pilar at the house at midday on the following Saturday, a whole week away.

"You will have an afternoon and one morning to talk to her, because I'll be flying back and arriving home for lunch on the second day." I thanked him profusely, and immediately set off on the long journey, the story of which could, on its own, fill half a book, but I think I've written enough about driving my old milk truck around the Americas.

11

Pilar: Wife to the Big Man

Pilar Wayne was lithe, slender and elegant, and I was surprised how young-looking she was, especially as a mother of three. With her thick, dark hair, pale alabaster skin and large deep brown eyes it was easy to see why Duke Wayne had been attracted to her. As we chatted, Pilar showed me around their beautiful seafront home, whose vast main living room overlooked the entire Newport harbour, where the yachts and their billowing red-and-white spinnakers sailing slowly past were a magnificent sight.

It wasn't a large house for a star of Wayne's earning ability – only four bedrooms – but a great deal of thought had been given to making it elegantly luxurious yet also restful and comfortable. The main rooms had quiet gold carpets that superbly set off the unusual antiques gathered from round-the-world trips – oriental art, especially from the Ming and T'ang dynasties. Ferns, rubber trees and oriental pot plants stood near the soft old leather settees and gave a soothing touch. There were Chinese tapestries on the walls, and ornaments from Thailand, Japan and China, plus fragile porcelain and stone horses from 900 BC and similar rare pieces. Pilar was proud of a red lacquer Chinese secretaire she had converted into a small bar, and there were many rare pre-Columbian objets d'art from Peru and Mexico. When I showed Pilar some of the photos I had taken in the museum in Mexico City she told me what they represented.

Wayne's own huge den at the back of the house contained his unique collection of Civil War miniatures, paintings and sculptures, plus nearly

300 cups, shields, plaques and framed citations from his many films and his work for the Marine Corps. His Oscar from *True Grit* held pride of place on his vast, dark desk, and his collection of rare Hopi Indian Kachina dolls from Arizona stood, dimly lit, on their own shelf. I thought that many a museum would envy the priceless treasures in the Wayne household.

Before I started my interview proper, Pilar took me out to their own jetty and their long sunny lawn, which stretched right down to the sea. Knowing that at that time the Wayne 'clan' included seven children and sixteen grandchildren, I asked her whether they ever visited. Pilar laughed: "Oh yes, the families visit when they can, individually, but once a year just after Christmas we hold an open house sort of family gathering when they *all* come at once, and some of their in-laws too. When we all gather for drinks on this lawn there are more than enough for two football teams!"

Pilar, actress daughter of a Peruvian senator, told me that when she and Wayne met on the jungle location of one of *her* films they had liked each other, but it wasn't quite love at first sight. She had been impressed by his height – he towered above those around him – by his air of quiet, confident authority, and by his wry smile, "which implied that while he was wise to the ways of the world and of women, he was gentleman enough to respect them but sometimes to ignore their stratagems!" When he flew back to Hollywood she admitted that she did wonder if she would ever see him again.

When her own film ended, Pilar was sent to Hollywood to do some soundtrack dubbing on it. Quite by chance she and Wayne bumped into each other in the Green Room restaurant at the Warner Brothers studio. Wayne remembered her instantly, and asked her to have dinner with him that night. "At first I thought it was just a kind of hands-across-the-Panama-Canal goodwill invitation, and I was, after all, twenty-three years younger than him. But I was alone in Hollywood, and I really liked Duke, so I accepted. I had dinner with him that night – and almost every night since! In fact I never went back to live permanently in Peru after that first dinner date. It wasn't long before we knew we were in love, and weren't happy when we were away from each other."

Duke never formally proposed to her, Pilar told me. One day he took her to see the rambling, beautiful old ranch house he owned in Encino, just outside Hollywood. It had twenty rooms, and nestled in its own secluded five acres of hills and wild woodland. It had a three-level garden, and a swimming pool down an enormous flight of stone steps. "As we stood in the driveway, Duke said, 'I bought this place in 1950. I've hardly lived in it … but if you don't think you'd be happy here, Pilar, I'll sell it and buy a smaller home wherever you like.' I just told him simply, 'I could be very happy here with you.' And that was the closest Duke ever came to making a formal proposal of marriage."

When she went with Wayne to Hawaii when he was making *The Sea Chase* with Lana Turner, she first discovered he could be full of surprises. September 3rd was her birthday, but as no-one even said "happy birthday" to her on that day in Hawaii, she felt rather low. Her first birthday away from home, and not even the man she loved remembered it! That afternoon, after they had been to a party given by the US Ambassador, Pilar was so unhappy she took off all her make-up and said she was going to bed. But Duke talked her into going for "a quiet bite to eat" at a restaurant called The Beachcomber.

"Knowing it was a rather dimly lit place, I just put on minimum make-up, not really bothering at all," she told me. Suddenly, as they walked through the door, a large orchestra was lit up and burst into 'Happy Birthday To You,' and one whole wall was decorated with flowers saying 'Happy Birthday, Pilar'. The cast and crews of two films were there, including some of Duke's dearest friends such as director Jack Ford, Ward Bond and Henry Fonda, all to help shower Pilar with congratulations.

"There was champagne, cake and presents, and all the time with hardly any make-up on I felt like a pale ghost. If I hadn't been so delighted that Duke had remembered my birthday after all, I could have murdered him!"

But Duke had far more romantic plans for Pilar in Hawaii. He was hoping against hope that his divorce decree from his second wife would become final in time for him to marry Pilar in a beautiful Hawaiian setting, preferably in a sunset. But filming gradually came to an end, and still there was no news. On their very last day, Duke and Pilar were having breakfast in their hotel when Duke's lawyer rang. "Your divorce is through," he said. "You're a free man!"

"Duke smiled at me with a huge grin. We both knew that was it. We were married the same night! The islands' judge came over at a few hours' notice to marry us, and Duke's film director John Farrow gave me away." And Duke got his other wish: it was a gorgeous, golden sunset on Hawaii's Kona Coast, with the sinking sun making what seemed a liquid path of gold from the heavens on the darkening sea, and the natives came along with instruments, leis and flowers and played *aloha* for the newlyweds

Pilar laughed at a memory: "Sometimes, if we have a little tiff, Duke pretends to be mad at me. He sighs, and kids me: 'You never even gave me one day of freedom. I was a married man at breakfast, single at lunch, and married again by dinner.'"

During the two days I spent with her Pilar gave me more fascinating insights into what it was like to be married to the world's greatest movie star. Despite his hellraising image and past she found him a totally committed family man. He was overwhelmingly generous, but this did not include throwing wild parties for his pals. His home really was his *home*, where his children could grow up normally and well adjusted.

She also soon realised that the real *raison d'être* of Duke's life was work. "He works harder than any man I've ever known. He has enormous energy, and can get by on four hours' sleep a night. Luckily, we both can. But he's not the tidiest of men to live with. He seldom puts things back in their places, and he often leaves his shirts on chairs and his socks on the floor where he's taken them off. And he's certainly no handyman. He can't hammer a nail or hang a painting. And he's no gardener. He can tell you where to hang a picture, or what colours to use in a room, as he has wonderful taste, but he can't do it himself."

After their marriage, both Duke and Pilar wanted their own children. Yet before the birth of each of their three – Aissa, Ethan and Marissa – Duke's concern for her always bordered on panic. "When Aissa was about to be born, I woke him up in the middle of the night and said we'd better start for the hospital, St Joseph's in Burbank. He kept saying 'Now, don't get nervous' as we got dressed. I wasn't at all nervous, but *he* was.

Driving me to hospital he kept singing songs off-key, the kind he used to sing with Ward Bond and Jack Ford around campfires on location in places like Utah. They were meant to calm me, I suppose, but they weren't those kind of songs at all! When Duke was first allowed into the hospital room to see his wife and new bouncing seven pound six ounce daughter, I thought he would say something beautiful and tender, something I would remember for years. But he just sat on the bed, wiped his anxious brow, and said, 'Move over, I'm pooped!'"

Pilar told me that for her it had been a case of marrying a movie actor and seeing the world, having been on his films in England, France, Japan, Hong Kong, Italy, Africa, Hawaii, Mexico and several other countries. But she seldom visited Duke's movie sets or watched his love scenes with his beautiful co-stars – not because she was jealous of him kissing other women for the camera, but because she felt in the way.

"He would like me to visit his sets more than I do. But I feel they're all working hard, and it's no place for me. If I sit in a chair it's almost always over a cable that has to be moved somewhere else. And if I'd watched his love scenes with a co-star like Sophia Loren I'm sure they would *both* have felt uncomfortable. It's *work*. He *has* to do it, poor fellow!" In fact, Pilar invited Sophia to their home for dinner. "Aissa was just a baby at the time, and we couldn't get Sophia out of our nursery. She hadn't had her own baby then, and I never saw anyone behave with a baby the way she did. She wanted a child so badly. I'm so glad she has her own little boy now."

The worst time for Duke and Pilar was when he was diagnosed with lung cancer at the age of 57. A heavy smoker since the end of his football days, he had developed a persistent cough, and Pilar finally persuaded her reluctant husband to have a check-up at the Scripps Clinic in La Jolla.

Duke himself had already told me of his initial shock at the diagnosis: "I felt as if someone had hit me across the gut with a baseball bat. I was scared, really scared, but I kept thinking more about my wife and kids, and did I have things in order for them? And how was I going to break the news to Pilar? So many things come into your mind, you don't have time to think about death itself too much." One thought that had plagued him was that even if he did get through the operation alive, he might be left a helpless invalid, with his loved ones feeling pity and sympathy for him.

He had the operation, and I now asked Pilar how she had felt during this awful period. She said that while she was terribly worried, she made sure she did not break down in front of Duke, as the last thing he needed was a tearful, overwrought wife. She did her best to remain optimistic and give him all the support, love and encouragement she could.

The doctors were satisfied with the operation, when most of his left diseased lung was removed, but soon afterwards oedema complications set in. Pilar, who spent every moment she could at Duke's bedside, recalled: "It was awful, because his face swelled up so much you couldn't see his eyes. One eyelid swelled up so much it covered almost half his face. Then that would subside and his neck would swell up. I was terribly worried then, and the doctors decided another operation was necessary."

Luckily the second operation was a complete success, and after a few weeks, when Duke felt well enough to sit up and watch TV, he wanted to go home. Pilar explained: "He didn't like the hospital routine, like being woken up at five in the morning to be handed a glass of iced water, or being isolated from his family. He was released into my care, and came home. I nursed him myself, as he didn't want a professional nurse in the house. His recuperation was supposed to last four months, but in fact he was up on his feet again inside two months. He was far from being a difficult patient. I had expected it to be far worse. For the first few weeks he was in considerable pain, but he didn't complain once. When his pal Henry Fonda visited, he quipped: 'This is the longest rest I've had in thirty years!'"

Pilar told me that what annoyed Duke most at this time was that his studio advisers had felt it bad for his 'heroic image' as a man who was larger than life that the world should know he'd ever had cancer. They released a story to the press that he had gone into hospital for an old ankle injury, and the surgeons had also removed an abscess from his lung.

"As soon as he was back on his feet, Duke called a press conference at our home and set the record straight. He hates lies of any kind. He told them his advisers had told him the public doesn't want its movie heroes associated with serious illnesses like cancer, as it destroys their image. He said he didn't care about 'images', and anyway he thought there was a lot better 'image' in the fact that John Wayne had had cancer and had licked it. I remember he paused a moment, then added: 'But I didn't beat it on my own, not without good doctors and the Man Upstairs.' He answered all questions, because he believed his own recovery might help encourage other people who got cancer. He also said more men should listen to their wives when they beg them to see their doctors. He told them it was I who talked him into getting that routine examination, and that I had probably saved his life!"

Pilar revealed more dramatic and humorous insights into her life with Duke, and at the end of that first day I knew I already had exactly the kind of material *Woman* magazine had wanted. When Pilar told me she worked to raise funds for various charities close to her heart, I promised her I would make her a sizeable contribution from any fee I was paid. (In fact, after the series was published, I sent her a cheque for $1,000.) I was so grateful, I also invited her out to dinner that night. To my delight she agreed, and said she knew a super small fish restaurant down in the harbour. She went upstairs to change her dress and get ready. I could hardly believe, even now, that I had not only spent the whole day in the luxury home of the world's biggest movie star but was now about to take his lovely wife out to dinner.

When Pilar came down, she looked even more graceful and elegant. She led me over the courtyard to their large garage, saying we could drive in Duke's car, and on the way take a look at his huge game-fishing yacht, *The Wild Goose*, now at anchor in the harbour. In the garage I saw what looked like a large Pontiac station wagon. Then we climbed inside. It was like getting into the cockpit of a modern jet. There were so many dials, switches and levers I couldn't find out how to even start the monster, never mind drive it. In the end, we had to send out for pizzas!

Later, Pilar offered me a spare bedroom, but I've never been able to sleep in strange houses, have never used a B&B in my life, and would also have felt ill at ease amid all the luxury. I thanked her – but spent the night in my old milk truck/camper parked in the Waynes' long drive.

My notebooks were even more full by the time Duke arrived at noon next day, having been driven from the airport by his manservant Fausto. Bearing in mind what he had said when giving me permission to visit his wife, after half an hour's more chat I was about to say my thanks and a polite goodbye, when both he and Pilar insisted I stay for the family lunch.

While the lunch was being prepared, Duke took me through his personal picture gallery. There were yellowing shots of a slim, rangy young Duke from the last days of the silent movies, with now-forgotten cowboy stars. "Yeah, I was a real skinny guy then," he laughed, in that voice that seems to boom up from a deep cellar. "For years I rode over most of the mountains west of Denver, doin' my own stunts for eatin' money." There were shots of Wayne with other stars, such as Clark Gable, Gary Cooper and Spencer Tracy, all dead and gone then. Suddenly he paused before a picture of his two strapping sons Michael and Patrick, striding along while he, taller than either of them, walked in front. He looked good in that picture, a big, proud, cocky grin on his face.

"Gee, that was ten years ago. I wish to God I looked like that now," he said. "Not for myself, but because of my work, the kind of parts I can play. I'd still like to play romantic leads, y'know, but hell, how can I at my age? I long ago gave up roles where I win beautiful women. A man has to know when to stop." He patted the slight paunch that protruded from the massive 244-pound Wayne physique, and the granitic face saddened. "Godammit, I hate getting old! You just can't do what you used to any more. I hurt this damn shoulder when I fell from my horse out in Louisiana. In the old days it would have taken ten days or so to heal up, but it's now more than a month and it's *still* giving me hell!"

I had a glimpse of what Duke was like as a father when Pilar called us in to lunch. As we sat down with the three children to an enormous tuna salad, little Marissa started to cry, saying that her older brother Ethan had taken her little brown book away from her. Pilar told her they would sort it out later, but right then they were eating lunch. Marissa kept whimpering, so Duke dropped his bread on his salad and got up to put things right. He established in fact that it *was* Ethan's notebook – he'd given it to him a week or two earlier, and it had Ethan's name on it. So Duke quietly told Marissa it was Ethan's, and therefore she must be mistaken. He went into his study and got her another notebook with *her* name on it. Then he came back to his lunch. I don't think many fathers would have reacted like that.

After lunch, and our cups of Sanka (decaffeinated coffee), I got my camera and asked Duke whether he'd mind posing for some pictures with Marissa and her little tricycle on the sun-filled patio, which overlooked the cerulean blue sea of Newport harbour. Before he came out, with a rueful grin he put on a yachting cap to cover up his baldness. "I don't care about it myself," he said. "Hell, it happens to a lot of men. But I don't see why I should inflict it on other people!" It wasn't vanity, because while he wore a hairpiece for his films and public appearances, in his normal life he never bothered.

After I thanked them both for their marvellous cooperation and hospitality, Duke walked me to my truck, and I asked him whether there was any little philosophy or maxim that he passed on to his children. "Well," he said, removing his cap and scratching his scalp thoughtfully: "There *is* something I tell the kids when they get to the right age – Don't judge other people unless you know the experiences they've been through. And only then if you truly *understand* those experiences."

As I drove away to Hollywood, to try and bag another star interview before the long slog back up to Canada, I thought that was really neat. But it was for a completely unintentional piece of advice that I came to most value my meetings with John Wayne. I had asked him how he felt generally about drinking.

"I never drink before 6 pm or sundown,' he growled, then added forcefully: "whichever is the *earliest*!" I have followed that smidgen of advice from that day to this, nearly forty years later. And it has stood me in very good stead.

12

Back to Britain — and Canada again

How and why I left Canada after three years in the wilds there was fully described in my book *Between Earth And Paradise*, so suffice it to say that it was after some thrilling treks to watch grizzly bears, bald eagles, cougar and caribou in their last remote fastnesses, including a fabulous trek with an inspiring old Scots-Indian called Tihoni, who taught me more by example than by word, that a strange sense of anticlimax had followed. Also, increasing numbers of city folk had discovered the beauty of my wild coast, and it was fast becoming a major vacation area.

By then I had finished my novel – the main initial reason for moving to Canada in the first place – and as its action took place mainly in Britain I would need to find a British publisher for it. Another good reason for leaving Canada was that I wanted to meet again the beautiful woman whose signing of a three-year filming contract that forbade her to marry for those three years had also helped to propel me off to Canada.

I sold my piece of land and log cabin to a keen young family who came stumbling along the rocky beach after they had looked at a too-costly bit of land with *no* cabin, further up the coast. My main worry was leaving my wild dog, Booto, who had 'adopted' me in my first log cabin winter. But he more or less solved the problem himself. Often, when he was bored by my long writing stints, or on my last trip south to meet John Wayne, when I'd had to leave him behind, he had often visited and stayed with Fred Jackson and his wife, and also with Stan and Julia Dimopolous, who owned the Seven Isles Cafe two miles up the coast. Both families agreed to look after him whenever he showed up – just as they had before he came to me.

Back in Britain, flattered at being remembered after so long an absence, I signed a contract as show business writer for a leading popular magazine, and moved into a smart flat in Knightsbridge. But my renewed romance with the woman I had loved fared little better than before, and I soon lost interest in the job and began to hate again the sheer racket of inner London. I had been a wilderness man for too long. I had learned to live in and love the wilderness, and it was time to move on again, and get back to it.

My long search for a new wild place, first in the Lake District and then in the Scottish Highlands, was well documented in *Between Earth And Paradise*, but it ended when I moved into a dilapidated old wooden croft on the Atlantic end of the island of Eilean Shona. After three and a half wonderful years there I moved to an old stone cottage halfway up a roadless, eighteen-mile-long freshwater loch I came to call Wildernesse. It was a truly wild place, set in sixty square miles of trackless mountain terrain, and it had no mod cons at all – no phone, TV, electricity or postal delivery. The only water supply was a plastic pipe from a burn, and the only access was by my small, open boat in all weathers. Yet it was here I intensified my exhaustive treks and studies on golden eagles, and eventually studied and bred rare Scottish wildcats, and even tamed one.

Four years after arriving in the Scottish Highlands I finished the long, complicated book about my adventures in Canada, which I called *Alone In The Wilderness*, and with high hopes I sent copies off to two top publishers. I was sure it would be readily accepted, so it was a shock when one sent it back with a note that they just didn't believe the story. They didn't think a thoroughly citified man (as I had been) could build himself a log cabin in the Canadian wilds, live mainly off the sea and, still less, trek out alone and camp out for weeks in dangerous grizzly country. I realised then that this would probably be the reaction of other publishers. As I had recently bought a camera and telephoto lens to record the wildlife around me, I felt I would have to get photographs of the wild grizzly and black bears, and much of the other rare wildlife I had encountered, and thus *prove* the book. When the Reader's Digest Press in New York *did* express interest in publishing the book, the need to get good photos seemed even more imperative.

At first I dickered with the idea of flying back to Vancouver, buying a new boat and engine, and re-creating my longest trek, some forty miles up a long sea inlet and river to fine bear country. The trouble was I had just started writing regular wildlife articles for the *Reader's Digest*, and after my years of financial parsimony I could not afford to be away for more than two, or at most three, weeks. And even if the boat and foot treks succeeded a second time, I could well be stuck back in Vancouver for a while, unable to resell the new boat and engine. I decided to try to hire a good guide, and accordingly wrote to everyone back in Canada who might help me find one. It was my old pal George 'Geordie' Tocher who came up with the goods. He sent me a magazine cutting about a leading Red Indian guide called Clayton Mack, who had guided hunters (mostly American) to kill a record number of the trophies that were now in the Boone and Crockett museum in New York. Geordie duly contacted Mack, and wrote to me that the guide would take me on a three-day trek to see wild grizzlies for a fee of $500. This was a lot less than the cost of a boat and engine, and made even more sense if I couldn't re-sell them fast.

A week later I flew to Vancouver. Geordie met me at the airport and took me back to his wooden cabin for the night, but not before a riotous time in a nearby beer parlour, where we were joined by one of his outback pals, big Ed McDermott. Big Ed had a raucous personality and an aggressive sense of humour, and started taking a delight in taking the mickey out of this Limey. I was starting to show my annoyance when Geordie drew me aside while Ed was harassing some men at the next table.

"Don't pick a fight with him, Mike. He likes nothing better, and has never lost a fist fight in his life!" I took another look at Big Ed. He was six foot four inches, weighed about seventeen stone, and moved like a big cat. I decided to take Geordie's advice, and just swallow the mickey-taking.

Next morning Geordie was due to drive me up to Williams Lake, where I was to meet the famous guide, Clayton Mack. Imagine my feelings when Big Ed turned up on the doorstep and announced he was going with us! We set off up Marble Canyon via Squamish in Geordie's battered old red pickup truck. It was a rough, un-made-up 'road', and with three of us on the bench seat in the cab I was squashed between the huge forms of Big Ed and Geordie, and couldn't recall a more uncomfortable ride. All the way up to near Lillooet the lads talked about sleeping out, 'under the stars', but ended up looking for a hut. We found one on the shore of Anderson Lake. They began gathering twigs and sticks, which Ed arranged in the primitive old grate to make a fire. Geordie had wasted over a dozen matches before I rearranged the sticks, suggested we needed some kindling (a word they'd never heard of), and gathered some dry moss and leaves from below a big tree, We then got the fire going. Big Ed treated me with more respect after that, but I was kept awake by his loud snoring.

Next day our riotous drive continued. We tried to buy some jade in Lillooet, which was famous for it, but couldn't find any. We drove on up via Pavilion, despite partially flooded roads due to a late spring run-off, to Clinton, a one-horse town, where the lads insisted we hit the beer parlour. A few beers later, and we set off to Seventy Mile House, where we hit another beer parlour, then on up to Hundred Mile House. There, feeling I really needed to take a grip on the situation, I insisted on buying Geordie dinner, but we left Big Ed still stolidly drinking in *that* beer parlour.

When we got back after dinner we found Big Ed talking to a tough-looking construction foreman called Rocky. Ed persuaded Rocky to take us all to his trailer home in a mosquito-ridden swampy area, eight miles out of town, where we discovered that Rocky had a very attractive, blonde wife. I told Geordie I *had* to get to Williams Lake and get some sleep, to be in better shape to meet Clayton Mack. Leaving Big Ed trying to get into bed with Rocky's wife, and Rocky too scared to do much more about it than talk loudly,* Geordie drove me up to Williams Lake. "I'll pick Ed up on the way back tomorrow," he said. We booked into a cheesy, cheap motel, and as I gratefully slipped between the sheets I re-member thinking: "I knew it. I should have flown up. My liver will hold

---

* A few years later, in similar circumstances, Big Ed was shot dead by an irate husband.

the scars of these past three days until the day I die." But I was still very grateful to Geordie for his kindness.

13

Danger among the grizzlies

Right from the start it seemed clear that I and Clayton Mack, the greatest wildlife and grizzly guide in North America, would not get along at all. As Geordie dropped me off in the bar of the Maple Leaf Motel in Williams Lake after our hectic night, I expected to meet a tall, tough, rangy bearded 'man of the mountains' type character. But the man who rose to greet me was very different. Clayton Mack was short, plump, wore thick-lensed glasses, and had a moon-shaped face wider than it was long, and bow legs that bore witness to his years as a champion rodeo rider. He walked like he still had a small horse between his legs! This was the best guide? Had I been conned by my contacts?

He had been on a three-day drinking binge, he admitted. "Are you okay for the $500?" was his first question. "Sure," I replied. "If we get grizzly. But how about $300 if we don't see any?" "Hell no! Five hundred dollars is the price. You pay if we see grizzly or no see grizzly." And he spat on the floor. He sure wasn't trying to please me.

Right then I felt like cancelling the whole trip, but I felt I would be letting Geordie down after he'd taken all the trouble to drive me up here. I just nodded to Geordie, winked, and said, "Looks like it's going to be fun!" He then set off to pick up Ed – "If Rocky hasn't shot him!" – and run them both back to Vancouver,

To my further unease, before we drove to Bella Coola in a large, battered, white sports car, Clayton crammed into it a good-looking Indian woman who, he said, was a legal adviser on Indian affairs in the Reserve, her two small daughters, and a boy who, after the first five

127

miles, was sick all over the back seat and the floor. As he drove along, Clayton confided that he had never driven the Plymouth Sebring before; he had bought it unintentionally the previous night while he was drunk. He had woken up this morning to find he had paid $5,300 for it, getting only $500 dollars back in return for his one and a half year old pickup truck, and the man who'd tricked him had vanished into thin air.

After about fifty miles we stopped, and Clayton asked me to take over the wheel, as he was very tired. I had never driven an automatic car before, but felt I had no choice. I set off down what was now just a rocky track. No-one could have called it a road. It had been built largely by amateur villagers from Bella Coola, who wanted a way out over land as well as by sea. The car's boot was soon an inch thick with dust, and the overloaded vehicle bottomed out over every slight bump, of which there was at least one every mile. It was 300 miles of sheer driving hell, and for much of the time all the others were fast asleep, leaving me to cope with every problem alone. I felt I must be crazy to undertake such a venture. When they woke up, they all started tucking into packed food and sucking at pop bottles, but none was offered to me, who was not only driving but also paying for everything!

Once, when we stopped at a trackside cafe shack to get some coffee, and I tried to talk Clayton into a better deal, he just said, "We will fight!" I said I had not come to fight, but to photograph grizzlies, and that I never fought unless I *had* to…. and left the rest unspoken. I took a very serious look at him, and reckoned that if it did come to a fight my first task would be to get his thick glasses off fast, as it would then be far more difficult for him to see what he was trying to hit.

Matters failed to improve when we reached Clayton's wooden cabin near the centre of Bella Coola. No arrangements whatever had been made for their new guest. When I asked where I could sleep, Clayton grunted, and pointed to a small, untidy living room. "There's a couch in there; will that be all right?" It was far too short for me, so I had to put three of its cushions on the floor and set my sleeping bag over them. No supper was offered either.

"I'm too tired to eat," Clayton told his squaw wife, never thinking to ask whether I might be hungry. And again, I was paying for all this. I felt it wiser not to protest, mainly because on the way in and looking out of the cabin windows I saw several very large, fit young Indian men walking about, two of whom came into the cabin to greet Clayton's return and to hear of his visit to Williams Lake. I was the only white man in the middle of an Indian Reserve. I went meekly to my 'bed' on the floor.

Next morning, as his wife started noisily washing up yesterday's dishes, there seemed no sign of breakfast – or even a cup of coffee. Eventually I said, in a loud voice: "Don't you eat breakfast here?" She replied, "I have ham and eggs in the fridge." She then went upstairs, woke Clayton, started cooking, and finally we had our ham and eggs. I felt better then.

The previous night Clayton had said we were to fly up to Quatna Inlet, where we would have to liaise with a Ken Stranahan, who was foreman of the logging camp there, which we would make our headquarters for the grizzly treks. But, as far as I could tell, he hadn't yet rung Stranahan.

I said I wanted to camp out, and not get mixed up in camp life, or in drinking sessions with the loggers. Clayton agreed, but said we should not camp out on or go near the tidal flats where the bears grazed or we might 'spook' them away, or they might attack us.

All morning we just seemed to bumble about: the local store was closed, so we had to drive twelve miles to find one in Hagensborg, and also for me to first pay in my $250 (half the total agreed fee) into his bank. At the store, Clayton said in a loud voice, "Choose what you like!", and seemed to make a show of himself paying the fifteen dollars for the groceries I'd chosen, as if showing he was paying for the white man!

Back at his home we rummaged around in his basement for over an hour, looking for a tent that wasn't holed and for a stove that worked, picking up one rusty relic after another. We walked to both his daughter's and nephew's houses to see whether either had a good stove, but had no luck. Finally we had to settle for a rusty, single-burner Primus pump-up model. To my suggestion that we didn't really need to cook anything anyway, apart from boiling water for tea, as we could subsist mostly on Polish sausage, bread, tomatoes, cheese and so forth, Clayton just grunted.

I then had to pack everything up to his car, as he said his back was bad. Up to now he hadn't seemed to do much for his $500, especially as I'd rung him ten days earlier to warn him of my coming. Although we would not carry a gun, Clayton showed me a small object that he said should guarantee us safety in the rare event of our being attacked, such as by a mother protecting cubs, or a bear stumbled upon unawares (usually the hiker's fault). It was a small naval flare device that he wore round his neck. It consisted of a short metal tube with a cartridge screwed onto one end. You pulled back the striking pin against a strong spring, let it go, and it would detonate a noisy, fizzing flare that bounced along the ground towards the bear. This would, especially if it hit the animal, turn the bear aside, giving us enough time to either scramble up a tree or drop face down into one of the many watery troughs that drained the tidal swamps. Well, I thought, a guide who had a record number of Boone and Crockett trophies to his credit must know what he's doing.

We then drove to his old leaking boat, baled it out, and extracted two pans, dishwashing liquid, a jar of jam, coffee, tea, and tins of beans, vegetables and milk. We loaded the new supplies into his car; then Clayton rang Wilderness Airlines, who said they could take us *now* to Quatna Inlet if we were ready. We drove to their floating launching ramp, and after I'd paid the $55 fare, and an alarming jolting short half-hour flight, we landed at the logging camp.

We were met by Ken Stranahan, who said his boat was ready for us. I was mildly annoyed when he and Clayton decided we would not tent out, but would stay in the last old shack of the logging camp. I did not argue, not wanting to risk offending these two men. We sorted out our rough bunks, set our supplies in place, and then Ken asked us to help get his boat into the water. I helped carry it, the oars and the 40 hp engine, and at exactly 6 pm we were on our way up the river, with Clayton at the helm.

It was my first experience of a 'jet boat', and I was amazed how the thrust of the burbling jet engine could propel the boat safely in, at times, a mere ten inches of water. There was a slight mishap after five minutes when the tiller handle came off in Clayton's hand and we had to go back for quick repairs, but as it was mid June we still had hours of daylight left.

130

We set off up river again, and after ten minutes came to a broad, slow-flowing area. Clayton turned off the engine so we could just drift along. It was suddenly silent and peaceful as the sun began to sink towards the high western ridges, but I now held my long telephoto lens at the ready, hoping to get shots of the great bears coming from the forests to their evening gratings on the lush grass and wild rice pastures that lay along the river banks. Clayton told me to grab the oars and pull into a high mud bank covered with swamp grass, where each leaf or stem was over an inch broad.

We climbed out and set off on foot through the waist-high grasses, red fireweed and skunk cabbage. Suddenly Clayton nudged my arms and pointed. There, in the mud among a trail of flattened grasses, were unmistakable grizzly tracks – like a man's, but far bigger and broader, some ten inches long and seven wide. Soon we came to thicker patches of skunk cabbage and purple-flowered wild rice plants, where a grizzly had been digging with its five-inch-long claws. I picked up one disinterred plant, and the soft, white grains spilled out from the thick cobby roots.

"Keep your eyes peeled," warned Clayton in a whisper. "Bears could have been here only minutes before."

I saw several trails of trodden-down grasses, and as we headed through the untouched areas, the undergrowth now almost armpit high, towards dark thickets of spruce, willow and alder, where long wefts of moss dangled from the trees, I felt really scared, that we were being watched by savage unseen eyes. We came across numerous broad trails that criss-crossed each other, and we moved cautiously. "Bears don't like rain too much, and there was plenty of it this morning," Clayton whispered. "They come out later in the sun and lie down in places like this, sunning themselves. We call them 'sun-out bears', and if you stumble on one 'cos you hadn't seen it in the high grasses, you're in real trouble!"

Now we came to a large, threshed flat area, which could have been caused by a sow playing with her cubs. Females don't usually breed until five years old; they have cubs (usually two) only once every two or three years, and don't breed after the age of eighteen in a maximum lifespan of some twenty-seven years in the wild. This, plus a high juvenile mortality (two thirds of grizzly deaths occur before the age of four and a half) means the recruitment rate is low. Sows usually run with their cubs for one and a half years, leave them alone in their second autumn, and mate the following June. Sometimes they run a third spring with the cubs, who are then driven off by the boar during mating. Now it *was* the mating season, and we had to be doubly careful not to disturb a boar with a sow, for the male is jealous and protective in these few days, and will charge at man or another interested boar.

Soon we were in the gloomy thickets below the spruce trees, and as I looked from one dark, secret abode to another, and saw freshly snapped stalks, Clayton sniffed the air. "I can smell them, like hogs, only sweeter," he said. I could smell them too, and my scalp prickled as again I felt we were being watched by hidden eyes. We found another threshed area, with clumps of grass torn up, which could have been caused by two boars fighting.

"It's not good in here. It's real scary, spooky in this swamp," Clayton whispered, and I could see from his fingers, which trembled like mine, that he was feeling the same heart-pumping sense of excitement and suppressed fear as I was. He had been mauled three times by grizzlies in his long career, and had suffered a broken vertebra in his spine, which still caused his left leg to go numb after some three miles of hard trekking. I felt that if *he* now felt nervous, I had good reason to be too! It was a sensation I'd first known in grizzly country seven years before when, hidden up a spruce tree, I had seen my first wild grizzly, a behemoth of a male, who had cantered into the clearing below me and sent some black bears hurtling up the nearest trees.

"It's not good in here," Clayton whispered again. "There are bears close to us. Let's keep near trees we can dodge round or get up." We headed for a small cottonwood and stood below it. All was silence for a while. Suddenly there came a flurry: across the clearing a sow bear and a young boar burst from the long grasses, scrabbled along a broad fallen log, the boar slipping slightly, and vanished over its far side. I took a shot, though the light was too poor. We waited a few minutes, then I heard a scrambling noise. Clayton was no longer beside me – he had climbed the tree.

"I'll take a lookout," he hissed; "see if there are any more out there." I waited two more minutes, feeling very alone and vulnerable at the foot of the tree, then scrambled up to join him. "What are you doing?" hissed Clayton. "I'll keep a lookout too!" I said. We waited a while, but there was no further movement anywhere, so we climbed down again and headed back for the boat, passing more grizzly prints in the mud, one of which was eleven inches long. Possibly the track of a big boar, it was following the line of the river.

We pulled out into midstream, shipped the oars, and let the boat drift in silence. Just round the bend I stood up slowly, camera ready, and saw him – a good 700-pound bear, with whitish muzzle and eye patches. He lifted a huge head above the grasses, sensing our presence, but with the wind from him to us he could not get our scent. I got two good shots before he vanished like a ghost into a thicket, having heard the click of the shutter at eighty yards. Further on we saw two cubs playing and rolling in the thick herbage, and a few yards beyond them their mother, scratching her back against a blackened stump. More photos, but the low sun was partly obscured by a mountain, and the light was poor.

After Clayton had regaled me with stories from his grizzly-hunting past, we spent the night on our bunk beds, back in the old shack on the outskirts of the log camp. I was startled at 5 am next morning to find Clayton shaking me awake, and to see that he was fully dressed. "I'm going up the track now," he said." Come on when you're ready and join me a mile up." At first I thought he was joking, but as I hastily dressed, and saw his squat, bow-legged figure dwindling and disappearing up the track between the giant trees, I knew he was not. I was a bit scared then.

Some of the loggers had told us they sometimes saw grizzlies on that track in early mornings, but that was always from their trucks. I was not in a truck; nor did I have that flare device that Clayton was carrying to scare off any aggressive bears. I set off up the dusty track, stumping along with my camera gear, and was even more scared when, after about a quarter of a mile, I saw a big grizzly head out of the woods on the right and cross the track at a slow saunter, followed by two big cubs.

I realised by now that Clayton was testing me, but cripes! What should I do now? I couldn't just funk it and head back to the shack, but I did wait for about five minutes between the trees. Then, feeling fairly sure the mother grizzly knew where she was heading, and wouldn't turn back, I nervously continued walking while keeping a sharp look out to my left. Clayton was sitting on a small knoll, from where he had been watching me. "I've just seen three grizzlies," he said, smiling for the first time, adding that he had seen them vanishing into a second belt of trees. It seemed they were the same bears that I had seen. Clayton was sure they were heading for the tidal meadows to graze.

We waited a while, then caught up with their tracks through the wood, coming to a fallen tree nearly three feet thick, where a huge hollow had been scratched out by bears digging for insects and grubs. Gingerly we crept towards the wood's edge, and there, out in the lush meadow, with the early sun glowing all into soft bright light, a glorious scene awaited us.

The mother grizzly and her two eighteen-month-old cubs were grazing before a tall willow filled with languid yellow flowers. Every so often she reared up on her haunches looking for danger, as I took shot after shot. Then, sensing our presence despite the favourable wind, she vanished with the cubs into trees on the far side. We cut west for half a mile, then saw a brown, moving hump in a small clearing. I took one shot, and the bear looked up and towards us.

"A young boar!" hissed Clayton. "Watch out. This one may come!" He was right. It did. It saw us, whirled in a half circle and then, with odd *ufu ufu* grunts, it charged. I managed one more photo, looked at the tree Clayton was climbing like a monkey, felt sure I'd never make it too, but with skinned hands and knees found myself up there beside him! The boar came only a few yards towards us, however, and then abruptly turned off and disappeared into trees on our right. It was a 'bluff charge', but frightening nonetheless. We waited several minutes, until we were sure the coast was clear, then retraced our steps back to our shack for lunch.

That afternoon, after I'd taken many scenic shots, and some of Clayton showing off, standing at the helm of the jet boat as it sped along, we cut the engine and let the boat drift along silently. After 200 yards we spied a huge boar grizzly, almost golden in the bright sunlight, grazing at the edge of a wood more than 500 yards away. There was no cover; only a few muddy sloughs running through the swamp.

"Do you want to get nearer?" asked Clayton.

"Not really!" I said honestly. "But I do want one really good close shot of a boar!"

We set off on foot, crouching so low through the sloughs that we could not see what the bear was doing. After 200 yards we cautiously raised our heads. It was still there, head buried in the herbage. Some ninety yards ahead was a small, tilted tree stump. Nerves tingling, we reached the stump, upon which I steadied the long lens. I got a shot of the boar grazing – a profile shot as it scented sideways into the cross-wind – then it was up on its hind legs looking straight at us, with a long piece of grass still dangling from its mouth. I took two more shots as we stayed stock still ready to drop flat, face down to the ground, should it charge. We had no hope of making it back to the river, nearly a quarter of a mile away, as a grizzly can cover 200 yards faster than an Olympic sprinter. But to our relief the big bear dropped to its feet and ran off into the forest. I got a few more photos, including one of three of the bears galloping along through the forested side of the river after being scared by our boat.

Back at the shack, knowing I'd got some fine photos, I pulled out the bottle of rye whisky Geordie had insisted on stuffing into my pack just before I'd left him. Geordie knew these hard men! Clayton smiled, for only the second time, as he took a big swig, and said, "I like you! You don't give a damn. You're not scared. I've had men shit themselves in places like that spooky swamp." I thanked him for the compliment, but said it was hardly the truth. I had been plenty scared!

More grizzly foot treks followed next morning, and in the end we had seen twenty-one wild grizzlies in two and a half days. "The most I've ever seen in that time," said Clayton, which I thought was quite an admission from a man who had the record number of twenty Boone and Crockett trophies to his credit. We had enjoyed a rare experience, even in what was one of the last three major strongholds of the bears in North America and Canada, for the animal was in slow decline. (I must add here that our treks were made in the years long before the now-famous grizzly-watching sites at the Neil River and Brooks Camp, Katmai, Alaska, were known to anyone but the local Indians.)

We caught the plane back to Bella Coola, where I gladly paid Clayton the further $250 I owed him, but he wasn't finished with me yet. "Okay, you've paid me for grizzly. Would you like some black bears as well?" I said, "Wow, I sure would!" Telling me to jump into his battered sports car, he drove me way out of town to the Bella Coola garbage dump. The whole area of the vast dump was suffused with smoke from numerous small fires started by garbage workers trying to reduce the amount of rubbish. To my amazement there were several black bears, two almost as big as small grizzlies, stumbling through the smoke and tunnelling into the piles of rubbish for anything edible.

Clayton said I could stand outside the car to use my tripod to take better photos, but to stay near it. The reason was that these 'dump bears' had largely lost their innate fear of man, and had been known to attack if, deceived by the bears' apparent tameness, humans went too close. I took fine shots of the black bears, and one of a huge 'Cinnamon bear', which was of a lighter colour, and which Clayton said Indians believed was a grizzly/black hybrid. I even took a few shots of a bald eagle, perched in a dead hemlock, which seemed to be waiting for the bears to leave a titbit or two.

Before we got back into his car, now our treks were over, I asked Clayton whether he would show me how his bear scarer worked – the little flare device he wore round his neck. "Sure," he said. He held the little tube out to his front, made some adjustment twist to the cartridge bit, pulled back the spring, and let it go. For agonising seconds nothing happened; then there was a tiny fizzing sound, a brief 'pop', and the flare just trickled out from the tube, dropped onto his boot, gave a final 'phut', and went out. If we *had* been charged by a bear it would have been totally useless. As he had no guns, we had been in mortal danger throughout!

When I bade goodbye to Clayton at the little airport next morning, I told him I'd got more than my money's worth. I flew back to Vancouver and found Geordie waiting for me with a big but slightly goofy smile. He'd had a couple of drinks, he explained, as my plane was almost an hour late and there was nothing else to do. What a pal! He shoved a bottle of San Miguel beer into my hand and announced we were going to a

Canadian strip club, as he knew I'd never been to one. I think I was more scared of what happened on stage that night than I was in the spooky bear swamp.

14

Farewell to Booto

After the dramatic grizzly treks with Clayton Mack, the most important task on my mind was to find and visit my old wild dog companion, Booto. For two days my phone calls to Stan and Julia Dimopolous, who owned the Seven Isles Cafe, went unanswered. Geordie told me that he thought Stan had died, and that Julia was running the cafe alone. Well, Booto could be with Fred Jackson and his wife, who had also said they would look after him. I borrowed Geordie's old Pontiac car, caught the ferry from Horseshoe Bay, and drove up the little coast road.

Fred Jackson's door was answered by a woman I had never met. She said the Jacksons had moved south to the small town near the ferry because, in their old age, they wanted to be near the hospital. She said she thought 'their dog' was now living up the coast at the Seven Isles Cafe.

When I reached the cafe it appeared deserted, the ground round it overgrown. The two side apartments were devoid of furniture. I climbed up the wooden veranda steps and saw that there were a few simple furnishings in the centre room – a table, two easy chairs, a sofa. It seemed someone *was* living there. I turned to look out over the rolling Pacific, the little tree-covered islets, the idyllic view that had once been mine from my own log cabin down the coast. I felt lost in the past.

Suddenly, there came a scraping on the wooden steps and an ancient, moth-eaten dog tottered towards me. This can't be Booto, I thought; it must be some old canine acquaintance of his, all power gone from once muscular rear quarters, the eyes dark, rheumy, filmy with age, peering at me with difficulty. The dog whuffed breathily as it moved, slowly, tired. Then it lay down as if sure I meant no harm, whoever I was.

Perhaps it *could* be Booto. I took out an old photo of him, taken in our palmy days together that seemed so long ago. I looked at the white boots on the feet, the chestnut ruff, the white patch on the chest – my god, it *was* Booto! All the past surged through my mind, how he had come out of a storm one February night when I had been wrestling with loneliness and the theme of a long novel I was writing, which was never published; how I had let him in and fed him, and his tail had wagged so vigorously that he could hardly keep his balance. I remembered all the comical tricks he used to get attention and food, how he had accompanied me on a hundred treks – had once lured a charging black bear with a cub away from me so that I could reach the cabin safely. I recalled our salad days in Hollywood, where he had learnt tricks so quickly that a magician had used him in his act at the famous Magic Castle Club. I remembered him on the film set near Durango, where I had gone to interview Dean Martin and Robert Mitchum, and Booto had run across in front of a shoot-out. The director, tough Henry Hathaway, had declared him to be the star of the scene! Back to my mind, too, the day I came to be the first man to run round the new Tartan track for the 1968 Olympic Games in Mexico City. And Booto had been the first dog, easily beating me over 200 metres!

Now, I lay down beside him and talked to the old, sleeping head. After a while he looked at me oddly, as if seeing me for the first time. Then slowly he raised his head, and his tongue, as pink as ever, licked my eye. There came a little moan of recognition, a slight wag of the tail. I broke down, sobbing bitterly, not for the past, not for the lonely years in Scotland without him before I found my promising young Alsatian Moobli, now being looked after by my best friend in the Highlands, but perhaps a little for the terror of old age. It was heartbreaking to see my companion, dear old Booto, reduced to such straits. The small sums of money I had sent to Julia Dimopolous to help feed him could not stem this onslaught of time. I had never felt so sad.

An hour or so later Julia returned from shopping, and Booto jumped up, glad to see her, burying his head in her lap, then in mine. He stood back, looking at us both, from one to the other, as if wondering anxiously what was going to happen now. Then, with an effort, he reared up and begged in his old inimitable way, one white paw comically folded over the other. I choked back my emotion and fed to him the pound of pure ground beef I had bought.

Booto had been a terror in his younger days, instantly attacking any male dog, irrespective of size, if he was with or after a bitch. He had been known as a canine Romeo, and over the years more than a few pups had borne an uncanny resemblance to him up and down the peninsula. Julia told me he still went 'courting', but in March had lost a battle with a bigger, much younger male dog, which tore his throat and lacerated his side. It had cost fifty-six dollars for the vet to patch him up. Julia said that she too was getting old, and would soon put the cafe up for sale. She hoped she could take Booto when she went to stay with her son Steve in Vancouver (she later did). I promised to give Booto's future some hard thought. With probably only a year or so to live, it was no good thinking of taking him back to the wilds of Scotland: he was at least 14, and battle-scarred into the bargain. Also, it seemed doubtful he would get along with young Moobli. But what I could do was to help Julia with more money for his keep.

Poor old warrior, I thought, as I looked at him. Old age makes us all so feeble. Death is the final onslaught of fatigue. I stayed a while longer, promised Julia I would write, gave Booto a clumsy hug, said goodbye and drove away.

Back in the Highlands, after picking Moobli up from my friend, I called in at Allan MacColl's village shop to replenish my supplies before the long boat journey up the lock to my remote home, Wildernesse. At the shop I was told that Allan had found two abandoned wildcat kittens, spitting and hissing in a ditch. He had managed to catch them, and was wondering whether I would like to have them, as they would be fascinating to study. I felt doubtful at first, but decided that at least I ought to pay him compliment enough to go and see them. Little did I realise then that ahead of me lay one of the greatest challenges of my naturalist's life – raising, studying and breeding rare, ferocious wildcats and releasing them back to the wild.*

---

* You can read all about that project in the new, revised edition of my book *Wildcat Haven*.

MY WICKED FIRST LIFE
Before the Wilderness

Mike Tomkies

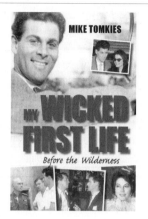

In wildlife circles, Mike Tomkies is a legend – called 'The Wilderness Man'. But here he tells the story of the very different first half of his life – before the wilderness years.

He describes his boyhood, both idyllic and traumatic, his first love of nature, and running away from home to join the Coldstream Guards where he became an army athlete and saw active service in Palestine.

He describes his provincial reporter years and progress to Fleet Street where, having landed a major scoop by gaining an interview with Ava Gardner, he was elevated into writing for a best-selling magazine's show business column.

From then on he flies the world – Paris, Rome, Vienna, Madrid, Hollywood – getting 'scoop' interviews with major stars.

His racy anecdotes about the stars he met are fascinating – Sophia Loren, Errol Flynn, Elvis Presley, Burt Lancaster, Kirk Douglas, Yul Brynner, Clark Gable, Dean Martin, Rock Hudson, Frank Sinatra, Jayne Mansfield, Cary Grant, Paul Newman, Joan Collins, Peter O'Toole and Sean Connery are just a few who either reveal some of their secrets or give him unusual encounters.

Tomkies describes how disillusionment finally sets in with both his work and himself – and why, at 38 he decides to start a new life and flies off to Canada.

'You would expect *My Wicked First Life* to be a name -dropping drive down memory lane, but it is much more. Tomkies' honesty with himself, as well as subjects, makes him a great writer.' *Border Telegraph*

And from the readers ...

'Your Autobiography is outstanding ... I pored over every word but can't make up my mind which one of your lives was the most exciting!'

'Your book ... what a life and what experiences! You certainly haven't held back – warts and all. It's great though – really enjoyed it.'

ISBN 978-1904445-35-7 234 × 156 mm 256pp 60 b/w photographs hardback £20

Alone in the Wilderness

Mike Tomkies

Mike Tomkies

The bestselling *ALONE IN THE WILDERNESS* tells the story of how Mike Tomkies left the hustle and bustle of city life as an international journalist over forty years ago and found a plot of land and rock in British Columbia, Canada, where he began a new life with only the basics – a tent and a typewriter!

How Mike built his log cabin, learned to live off the sea, adjusted to the demands of Nature – the hardest taskmaster of all – makes exciting and informative reading. If you have ever wondered what it *really* feels like to be away from the pressures of modern life, this is the book to read. Mike shares the high and lows of this rare escapist experience. The variety of animals that he encountered, including bald eagles, a cheeky raccoon, grizzly bears, killer whales, cougar are all keenly observed. Three extraordinary characters enhanced his experiences there: Ed Louette, a backwoods carpenter of sculptor-like skill; Pappy Tihoni, a Scots-Indian of uncanny animal sense; and wild dog Booto, who scratched at his cabin door when loneliness threatened to overwhelm. It is also a story of a man in search of himself and is a compelling account of his wilderness days.

'Wonderfully written, it is as entertaining as any novel and also introduces some wildly eccentric characters – Ed Louette, a backwoods carpenter extraordinaire, and Pappy Tihoni, a Scots-Indian possessing a remarkable, Tarzanesque affinity with the animal population.' *Yorkshire Post*

'Tomkies is to be congratulated on a splendid book. His feelings for people, animals, wilderness are expressed honestly and beautifully. His descriptions of nature are sensitive as well as accurate and image-provoking.' *Dr. Victor H. Cahalane, former Assistant Director, New York State Museum*

'The life it portrays, the nerve and daring it reveals, can only inspire in most of us, slothful dreamers that we are, feelings of respect and envy.' *Natural History Magazine*, New York

ISBN 978-1870325-14-1 192 pp 240 x 170 mm colour photographs £18.99

Whittles Publishing • Dunbeath • Caithness • Scotland • UK • KW6 6EY
Tel: +44(0)1593-731 333; Fax: +44(0)1593-731 400;
e-mail: info@whittlespublishing.com; www.whittlespublishing.com

VHS Videos & DVDs from Mike Tomkies

EAGLE MOUNTAIN YEAR (125 minutes, VHS video for £15, DVD for £10)

This tape tells the story of a magical Highland mountain through all four seasons. There are golden eagles at the nest, their glorious courtship 'air dances', and a female eagle hauling a deer carcass uphill on her own. Rare black-throated divers are seen diving, courting and, for the first time on film, at their nest. Pine martens are shown hunting, at their den, even feeding from my hands. Hunting and nesting peregrine falcons are shown in detail, as is all the comic-tragic sibling rivalry at buzzard nests. There are courting mergansers, ospreys, ravens, foxes and even a hunting wildcat. Throughout all, I show the lives of the red deer herds.

AT HOME WITH EAGLES (102 minutes, VHS video for £14 , DVD for £9)

Shown in incredibly intimate detail, this is the story of three pairs of courting, hunting and nesting golden eagles – one pair exchanging incubation duties, a second pair trying against the odds to hatch infertile eggs, and a third pair who are success-ful in raising their chick from egg to flying stage. Never before have the secret lives of the king of birds been revealed in such fascinating detail. Two eminent naturalists have described it as *'probably the greatest eagle film ever made.'*

FOREST PHANTOMS (60 minutes, VHS video, £9)

This tape takes six barn owls through a full year, from chicks to hunting adults. Also starred are the forest phantoms of the day – rare goshawks at the nest, as well as nesting buzzards, long-eared owls, foxes, and, yes, even eagles again.

MY BARN OWL FAMILY (52 minutes, VHS video, £8)

A tape of my barn owls Blackie and Brownie, and how they finally raised four youngsters to flying stage. We see them incubating eggs, hunting the woods and pastures, perch hunting from my garden fence, and taking prey back up to the loft. Intimate glimpses of their complicated behaviour inside the loft and nest box; and all the growing stages of the chicks are recorded in loving detail. Also shown are the daytime 'invaders' of their world – a badger who was unusually tame, a fox who used my sheep walls to spy prey, a beautiful female kestrel who came for any food the owls left on the table – not to mention chaffinch hordes, bellicose siskins, cheeky jays and other entrancing characters.

RIVER DANCING YEAR (92 minutes, VHS video, £13)

A celebration of the superb wildlife of Scottish rivers – from the raging upper water-falls where salmon leap heroically to reach their spawning grounds; through serene reaches where swans, herons, moorhens, mallards, dippers, goosanders, gulls and kingfishers go about their lives and finally to where the river enters the sea and the estuary kingdom of the great sea eagles. We see foxes playing in a riverside garden, a vixen giving suck to her four cubs … a boisterous badger family, digging, playing hilarious judo games, and even taking food from my hands … a grooming, prowling and hunting wildcat … otters fishing and in their holt … peregrines guarding their chicks … herons catching fish and even swallowing a duckling, a young golden eagle preparing to leave its nest … ospreys catching and bringing fish to their grown young … and a host of other species. Above all, it is a long insight into the world of the rare white-tailed sea eagles, as a pair guard their flown youngster, exchange beak-to-beak greetings, and provide glorious flight sequences when they hunt for prey in their kingdom at the end of the river.

WILDEST SPAIN (77 minutes, VHS video, £10)

A tape about Europe's finest wildlife. It tells of successful treks and adventures all over Spain in pursuit of wild bear, wolf, lynx, wild boar, ibex, black stork, very rare vultures and eagles, plus many other species in a magical European country not hitherto known for its often excellent wildlife conservation.

WILDEST SPAIN REVISITED (52 minutes, VHS video, £9)

This updates the previous video, with totally new material, concentrating on rare wild brown bear and wild wolves. Some extraordinary and hitherto unknown behaviour is captured.

LAST EAGLE YEARS (75 minutes, DVD, £6.50)

This tape covers the five wilderness years since all the previous videos ended. I show three pairs of hunting, courting and nesting golden eagles, a veritable feast of red kites competing with ravens, buzzards and crows for food, and goshawks and peregrine falcons at the nest. There are wild goats (and a fight between two males), brown hares, courting curlews, red and rare black-throated divers, and a long sequence of ospreys hunting for fish and feeding young at two nests. On my way to the kingdom of the rare white-tailed sea eagles, I show huge Atlantic seals and dolphins somersaulting in the sea, and finally the great sea eagles soaring to and from their island nest as they tend their single youngster.

MY BIRD TABLE THEATRES (80 minutes, DVD, £6)

This tape showing the fascinating behaviour of the myriad hordes of birds who visited bird tables at my last four homes, ranging from the wild Scottish hills near Ullapool, to the Borders and deepest Sussex. Shown through the four seasons, all the normal garden birds are here plus nuthatches, linnets, goldfinches, ring doves, colourful jays, green woodpeckers, comical squirrels, a flock of pheasants who became tame, and even a kestrel and a barn owl. At night foxes and a pair of badgers come for the food

I set out, including a huge semi-albino boar weighing over 30lbs who pulls down a Victorian pedestal a man can hardly lift, to get at some meat.

MY WILD 75th SUMMER (80 minutes, DVD, £7)

My last season filming peregrine falcons, red kites and goshawks feeding chicks at the nest; the roe deer, foxes and cubs, and a badger pair at my new wildlife reserve in deepest Sussex. It shows how I set up the reserve, planted a wild flower meadow and the butterflies it attracted. I show the playful and courting behaviour of rabbits, foxes, squirrels, pheasants, plus jays feeding flown chicks, a frolicking weasel and colourful woodpeckers. The film ends with fabulous footage of rare white-tailed sea eagles soaring to and from their tree nest on Mull with prey, and how they cooperate to feed their twin chicks.

MY WILD 80th YEAR (92 minutes, DVD, £7)

This DVD shows all the super wildlife action at my little wildlife reserve. It starts on my 79th birthday with a magnificent golden eagle on my arm. It shows the slow taming of a huge wild badger who comes into my house to pull his feed pan from my hands, barn owls hunting my paddock, the fascinating nesting and courtship behaviour of great crested grebes on a nearby lake, great spotted woodpeckers in and out of their nest hole, green woodpeckers anting, colourful jays bathing and burying acorns, and many small birds feeding from my hands. Also included are two trips to Scotland for nesting and hunting ospreys, and rare Slavonian grebes nesting amid beautiful water lilies. It ends with a fierce goshawk feeding from a rabbit it killed and from a cock pheasant it struck down in flight, and falconer, Neil Hunter, bringing his superb golden eagles to my garden for a memorable day.

Books

GOLDEN EAGLE YEARS (£10)

The re-issue of the book long out of print, which contains more and better colour pictures than the first edition. It tells of my first five years studying Scotland's magnificent golden eagles. The treks, the pitfalls and defeats, the joys and triumphs, are fully described.

Please send your remittance and delivery address to:

Whittles Publishing Ltd, Dunbeath Mains Cottages, Dunbeath, Caithness, KW6 6EY, Scotland. (Cheques payable to Mike Tomkies*)*